Industrial Democracy
in Western Europe

A NORTH AMERICAN PERSPECTIVE

Industrial Democracy in Western Europe

A NORTH AMERICAN PERSPECTIVE

Professor John Crispo
Faculty of Management Studies
University of Toronto

McGRAW-HILL RYERSON LIMITED

Toronto, Montreal, New York, St. Louis, Auckland,
Beirut, Bogotá, Düsseldorf, Johannesburg, Lisbon,
London, Lucerne, Madrid, Mexico, San Francisco,
New Delhi, Paris, San Juan, São Paulo, Singapore,
Panama, Sydney, Tokyo

INDUSTRIAL DEMOCRACY IN WESTERN EUROPE:
A North American Perspective

ISBN 0-07-082700-1

1 2 3 4 5 6 7 8 9 10   AP   7 6 5 4 3 2 1 0 9 8

Printed and bound in Canada

Canadian Cataloguing in Publication Data

Crispo, John H.G., 1933-
Industrial democracy in western Europe

ISBN 0-07-082700-1 pa.

1. Employees' representation in management.
I. Title.

HD5650.C75   658.31'52   C77-001703-7

TABLE OF CONTENTS

	Page
Preface and Acknowledgements	**1**
Chapter 1 — INTRODUCTION	**5**
Collective Bargaining — The Traditional Model	5
Alternative Approaches and Emphases	7
The Ferment in Western European Industrial Relations	8
Approach and Scope of the Study	10
Outline of the Volume	12
Chapter 2 — INDUSTRIAL DEMOCRACY: ITS MEANING AND RATIONALE	**13**
Collective Bargaining and Industrial Democracy: The North American Model	15
Beyond Collective Bargaining: The Western European Experience	16
The Growing Interest in Industrial Democracy	18
Union Ambivalence	21
Employer Concerns	23
Government Interest	24
The Process and the Results	26
Chapter 3 — INDUSTRIAL RELATIONS IN NORTH AMERICA AND WESTERN EUROPE: SOME BASIC CONTRASTS	**27**
Industrial Relations in North America and Western Europe	28
The Environment	28
The Parties of Interest	32
Interaction Processes	36
Results	38
Variations Within North America	38
Variations Within Western Europe	40
The Perils and Pitfalls of Generalizations	43

**Chapter 4 — COLLECTIVE BARGAINING IN
WESTERN EUROPE**   **44**

Competing Forces and Conflicting Trends in Western European
    Collective Bargaining   45
The Italian Variation   48
The Swedish Variation   49
Future Developments   51

**Chapter 5 — ORGANIZED LABOUR AND NATIONAL
ECONOMIC AND SOCIAL POLICY FORMULATION**   **53**

Limitations on Organized Labour's Participation in National
    Economic and Social Policy Formulation   54
Alternative Forms of Union Influence in National Economic
    and Social Policy Formulation   55
Britain's Social Contract   58
The Netherlands' Situation   61
Austria's Parity Commission on Prices and Wages   63
West Germany's Concerted Action Committee   64
Belgium in a State of Flux   66
Form and Substance in France   67
The Swedish Variation   67
Conclusion   69

**Chapter 6 — JOINT OR TRIPARTITE ADMINISTRATION
OF SELECTED PUBLIC PROGRAMS**   **71**

Western Europe's Tripartite Labour Courts   72
Manpower and Social Security Administration in West
    Germany   73
Sweden's National Labour Market Board   74
Britain's Advisory Conciliation and Arbitration Service   76
Developments in Other Countries   77
Conclusion   78

**Chapter 7 — WORKER REPRESENTATION ON
COMPANY BOARDS**   **79**

Unitary and Two-Tier Company Boards: A Distinction
    of Varying Significance   81
Codetermination in West Germany   83
    The Montan or Coal and Steel Model   84
    The New Compromise Codetermination Law   86
    The One-Third Model of Codetermination   87
    An Overall Appraisal   88

The Netherlands Version — A Case of Mutual Veto Rights   90
Britain's Bullock Report   92
Developments in Other Countries   95
The Role of the European Economic Commission   97
Continuing Issues and Problems   99
  The Ideological Spread in Viewpoints   99
  Delays, Compromises and Politics   100
  Union and Worker Conflicts of Interest   101
  Unitary or Two-Tier Boards   101
  The Power of Supervisory Boards   102
  The Proportion of Worker Representatives on
    Company Boards   103
  Relationship to Other Forms of Industrial Democracy   103
  Degree of Union Control Over Worker Representatives   104
  The Responsibility of Worker Representatives   105
  The Question of Public Representation   105
  The Question of Management Representation   106
  Elitism and Formalism   107
Conclusion   108

Chapter 8 — WORKS COUNCILS   **110**
The Position of Works Councils   111
Works Councils — Traditional Weaknesses   114
Works Councils — Some Recent Developments   115
Future Prospects   118

**Chapter 9 — OTHER ISSUES, PROBLEMS
AND PROSPECTS**   **119**
Worker Asset and Capital Formation Plans   120
  Profit and Share Participation in France   121
  Government Encouraged Worker Savings and Investments
    in West Germany   121
  Denmark's Proposed Wage Earners Investment and
    Profit Fund   122
  The Meidner Plan in Sweden   123
  Control Over Pension Funds in Britain   125
  Conclusion   126
Shop-Floor Democracy and the Quality of Working Life   126
Information and Confidentiality   128
Education and Training   130
The Multinational-Corporation Complication   132
Industrial Democracy in the Public Service   134

**Chapter 10 — INDUSTRIAL DEMOCRACY AND
THE FUTURE OF LABOUR AND MANAGEMENT**   **136**
Trade Unions and the Corporate State   137
The Future Role of Management and Managers   141
The Pressing Need for a New Managerial Style   141
Whither Management Representation?   144
A Note on Labour Directors and Their Equivalents   147

**Chapter 11 — IMPLICATIONS AND RELEVANCE
FOR NORTH AMERICA**   **149**
Reforming North American Collective Bargaining   150
National Economic and Social Policy Consultation   153
Labour and Management and Public Administration   156
Unions and Workers and the Composition of Company
Boards   157
An Alternative to Works Councils   160
Organized Labour and Pension Plans   161
Humanizing Work and/or the Work Place   162
Education for Industrial Democracy   164

Chapter 12 — SUMMARY AND CONCLUSION   **165**
The Prerequisites for Effective Forms of Industrial Democracy   167
The Road to Industrial Democracy   170
The Choices Ahead   172

Selected Bibliography   175

Index   177

PREFACE AND
ACKNOWLEDGEMENTS

Industrial relations has always been the focal point of my work because it is such a central part of our total socio-economic-political system. Although some might argue with this proposition in North America, it is an indisputable fact of life in Western Europe. There this interrelationship is becoming ever more salient and telling, as union and worker influence in decision-making at all levels of society increases.

Previous visits to Western Europe had made me aware that industrial relations in most countries on the continent has long embraced much more than collective bargaining. Indeed, one could argue that industrial relations itself has now become part of an even larger umbrella concept known as industrial democracy. Regardless of the terminology used, the point is that Western Europe is permeated by examples of new ways in which unions and workers participate in decision-making in numerous areas heretofore in the exclusive domain of management or government or some combination of these or other interest groups.

My interest in these developments was whetted by the growing but still comparatively ill-formed nature of the debate about industrial democracy in Canada. There have been muted sounds about this notion for years, but only recently has the subject been more widely discussed. In large measure the popularity of the topic has been brought about by the search for a way in which to rid Canada of the wage and price controls which were imposed on the country in October 1975. One of the responses of the labour movement in Canada was to issue a manifesto calling for more tripartite decision-making at the national level.

Meanwhile senior labour department officials, especially at the national level, but also under some provincial auspices, have begun to lend their support to the cause of industrial democracy in one form or another. Aided and abetted by the media which appreciate even less about the subject than those issuing pronouncements on it, the cause has been pursued to the point where it could become an irreversible force before there is a full understanding of what it is all about or what is at stake.

If only for my own sake, but hopefully for others as well, I decided to try to discover what is entailed by industrial democracy in Western Europe. Taking advantage of two previous trips and numerous contacts developed during those visits, I decided to return again on a more extended basis to as many countries as I could. My purpose in each case was to bring myself up to date on the latest developments in industrial democracy in each of these countries. Based on these individual country surveys, the idea was to get an overview of the general situation in

Western Europe, which then could be related to the North American scene.

Throughout this exercise I have been extremely leery about the transferability of the successes in one country's industrial democracy to another's. Attitudes and institutions and many other features vary too much between different countries to permit anything like direct transplants between them. This is not to say, however, that one country cannot learn from another nor adapt some of its own practices on the basis of fruitful experiences elsewhere. This is the spirit in which I have approached this project.

I am indebted to so many individuals and institutions for assisting me in this undertaking that I cannot hope to acknowledge all of them. I am grateful to my Faculty and University for a long overdue sabbatical leave, and to the Canada Council for financial assistance during my leave. I also appreciate the support afforded me by the Canada Department of Labour during the summer I spent after my leave writing this volume.

While on leave two institutions generously offered me the use of their facilities for several months. I was a Visiting Professor at the London Graduate School of Business Studies during the Fall of 1976 and a Visiting Scholar at the International Institute for Labour Studies in Geneva during the Winter and Spring of 1977.

Most of my leave was spent interviewing labour, management and government representatives, as well as academics and officials of international agencies. Almost invariably, these individuals gave unsparingly both of their talent and of their time. This study would have been quite impossible without their generous cooperation.

Among those who commented most helpfully on the first draft of this volume were Roger Blanpain, Director of the Institute for Labour Relations at the University of Leuven in Belgium, Robert Coleman from the Economic and Social Affairs Directorate of the Commission of the European Communities in Brussels, and Jacques Monat from the International Labour Organization in Geneva. Especially constructive were the suggestions made by Paul Malles of Ottawa who also helped inspire this undertaking in the first place, and George Haines, a colleague at the University of Toronto, who reviewed the manuscript from an editorial point of view.

I alone, of course, must bear the ultimate responsibility for any errors of fact or interpretation which remain.

March, 1978   John Crispo

Chapter 1

INTRODUCTION

This volume is an outgrowth of growing concern about the state of some of North America's basic industrial relations institutions. The fundamental issue is whether collective bargaining as it has been traditionally practiced in North America can survive. To come to grips with this question even tentatively requires an assessment of the burgeoning alternative approaches which have emerged in Western Europe.

Attempting to review these developments is a difficult task because they are so selective, varied, and, above all, fast-moving. In comparison with the relative stability of the North American industrial relations landscape, that of Western Europe represents a kaleidoscope of change. This rapidly shifting labour relations scene reflects an underlying trend towards more union and worker influence in all levels, manners and types of decision-making.

COLLECTIVE BARGAINING:
THE TRADITIONAL MODEL

Collective bargaining may be described as a means through which workers have jointly sought to resolve their differences with their employers. Employees have gained power by combining together in unions to achieve everything from higher pay to enhanced job security. The assumption is that there is a natural division of interests between employees and employers. Workers tend to have little or no say in the resolution of these differences in the absence of collective bargaining.

Because collective bargaining deals with such divisive issues it normally gives rise to adversarial relations. Moreover, failure to reconcile such issues through negotiations usually leads to a confrontation in the form of a strike or lockout. More often than not it is the threat of the strike or lockout, if not the eventuality of one or the other, that makes the process work. Industrial conflict is thus not necessarily to be seen as an aberration or breakdown in the system, but rather as a critical catalytic agent.

As conventionally conceived, collective bargaining entails a process of challenge and response. Employers manage in accordance with their perception of their rights. This becomes a challenge to unions and workers when they have a different viewpoint. Accordingly they must fashion what they deem an appropriate response. Collective bargaining thus becomes a bipartite series of challenges and responses marked by periodic power struggles and realignments of positions.

The role of the state in this type of collective bargaining system need not be that great. Basically all that governments have to do is provide for the rights of unions to exist and take effective action, to lay down the reciprocal rights and responsibilities of labour and management, and to protect the public interest when the behaviour of either or both parties threatens to do real harm.

The problem with this supposedly limited role of the state is that it can be interpreted in a highly interventionistic manner. Under the guise of one public interest or another, governments can rationalize all sorts of interferences in the collective bargaining process. What is meant to be essentially a bipartite system can, thus, quite readily become a tripartite one or even one dominated by the state.

When traditional collective bargaining becomes something quite different is a highly debatable point. No doubt the dividing line occurs when the state feels compelled to interfere in more and more industrial disputes by imposing settlements upon the parties. As this happens the right of labour and management to chart their own destinies through collective bargaining is clearly threatened.

ALTERNATIVE APPROACHES AND EMPHASES

Either with or without a push from the state the collective bargaining process could move in any number of directions. It is most useful for present purposes to examine the impetus for change stemming from unions and workers. Employers generally favour the status quo if only because they believe any changes are likely to run contrary to their interests. Unions and workers really have three basic choices when it comes to collective bargaining.

The first of these choices may be termed the North American or business union option. Fundamental to this alternative is the willingness to accept collective bargaining as an integral part of the capitalistic, enterprise or market system, but only so long as organized labour is as free as every other group to charge what the traffic will bear. Acceptance of this approach need not entail the total absence of any commitment to reform of the overall socio-economic-political system, but any such reform instincts are limited to relatively modest changes and not to revolution or transformation.

At the other end of the spectrum of possible union and worker responses to the collective bargaining process are those ideologically committed to a new social order and society. Such groups are a major force to be reckoned with in several Western European countries, where they completely reject the existing system and therefore have at best an ambivalent attitude toward collective bargaining. On the one hand, they are tempted to renounce it completely as part of the overall system they are dedicated to replace. On the other hand, they are compelled to work within it as long as it persists, if only to extract sufficient material and other gains to maintain the support of their members.

Between these two extreme union and worker responses to the collective bargaining process is another set of possibilities which is difficult to delineate or label. Simplistically the unions and workers which fall into this category might be termed consensualists, collaborationists or integrationists. But these terms suggest a degree of cooptation or integration and even selling-out, which later discussion will reveal is quite inappropriate. This element of the labour movement rejects neither conflict nor basic change. It prefers, however, to seek both day-to-day improvements in the lot of workers and modest reforms in society by a variety of means, including (but only including) collective bargaining.

This is what this volume is all about. Collective bargaining as originally conceived is only one means by which unions and workers can influence what goes on at the industry, firm or plant level. So too, political action, which has thus far not been mentioned, is but one avenue by which unions and workers can influence decision-making beyond the enterprise level. Recent Western European experience reveals that there are a wide variety of hitherto unexplored channels through which unions and workers can participate in a meaningful way in decision-making at all levels in the socio-economic-political system.

THE FERMENT IN WESTERN EUROPEAN INDUSTRIAL RELATIONS

The rate of change in Western European industrial relations has been rapid in the past few years. The ferment that continues to characterize Western European labour relations can be said to have begun during the French crisis of confidence in 1968. From 1968 until at least 1971 almost every country in Western Europe experienced its own milder variation of the turmoil that plagued French industrial relations after the student demonstrations there almost provoked a revolution.

Although no country in Western Europe experienced anything quite like the French trauma, all saw some of their long-established institutions challenged. Especially noteworthy in the industrial relations arena was the fact that unions were as much the subject of these challenges as any other bodies. Years of relatively stable union-management relations had to give way to a more turbulent period as unions sought various ways of responding to their members' apparent disillusionment with them. It is not surprising that both unions and employers were driven to explore new ways of conducting their relations in the face of everything from unofficial and unauthorized wildcat strikes, through plant sit-ins and work-ins to enterprise seizures.

The response to this crisis of confidence on the union side was naturally mixed. The major union thrust in many countries involved more emphasis on company and plant level bargaining to supplement the more customary national or regional negotiations. In many of the same countries greater priority was given to flat across-the-board increases which appealed to the mass of workers because of their income-levelling effects. There was also a pronounced development of non-monetary demands in most countries, accompanied by a rise in the more conventional wage and salary and fringe benefit claims. This shift in emphasis took the form of more emphasis on codecision-making powers at all levels of society in some countries — including Britain, the Netherlands and Scandinavia. Various types of schemes to promote shop-floor democracy and an improved quality of working life also gained prominence in several countries.

All of these developments are still continuing and it is much too early to discern the eventual results. Nor is there much sign of any significant letup in the pace of change in many countries. Just as the situation seems to settle down in one country, another series of innovations breaks out in a neighbouring country. Although little or none of this rotating change of pace can be attributed to a domino effect, there is no doubt that Western Europe's gradually increasing interdependence has had its impact on industrial relations, as well as other important aspects of life within each of the countries involved.

The problem for a student of industrial relations in Western Europe is to try to keep abreast of the situation in each country. As will be repeatedly stressed, this book deals with generalities and consequently may be less vulnerable to this problem than would otherwise be the case. Unfortunately it still cannot be denied that despite reliance on interviews with individuals who are in the midst of the latest developments in their countries, this study is bound to be dated almost as fast as it is being written. This is the inevitable price to be paid for writing on a subject as fast-changing as Western European industrial relations.

APPROACH AND SCOPE OF THE STUDY

This volume may best be characterized as an editorial and impressionistic essay. Aside from the author's predisposition to favour this form and style there are many other reasons for such an approach. First and foremost is the desire to provide a readable text uncluttered by the numerous qualifications and references which would have to be included in a more academic treatise. Secondly, a traditional scholarly approach is really inappropriate since there has been no time yet to assess the results of many of the developments discussed here. Moreover, much of the research which has been undertaken so far has concentrated on descriptions of the institutions and laws involved. There has been surprisingly little definitive work done on the impact of any of Western Europe's ventures in industrial democracy, especially at the rank and file union member or worker level.

Aside from the lack of hard data and facts, the subject matter of this essay suffers from little neutrality of viewpoint, let alone anything approaching objectivity. To put it another way, there are few areas of study nowadays which are plagued by more highly opinionated, ideologically charged, or politically motivated viewpoints. Personal philosophy is not only the overriding consideration for the labour and management participants in the processes under investigation, but for outside commentators and observers as well.

Because of the subjectivity that invariably encroaches upon an analysis of this kind, it is only fair that the author should reveal some of his own biases. For the most part these revolve around a commitment to a hierarchy of values and institutions which may well be on the losing end of world trends. At the top of this hierarchy of values and institutions is freedom itself. Freedom in this sense primarily includes freedom of speech and freedom of association. But it also includes both freedom of contract and property and the necessary quid pro quos for the latter; that is, equality of opportunity and freedom from human degradation, poverty and suffering. Second in this hierarchy of values and institutions is liberal democracy, whether congressional or parliamentary in form or some combination of the two. Regardless of the form which it takes liberal democracy embodies an electoral system under which the people of a nation freely elect those who are to preside over them within well established constitutional limits. Third, and much more controversial, is mixed free enterprise or modified capitalism. This system has, to date, proven to be the only economic system compatible with the maintenance of liberal democracy and freedom. Such a market economy may vary in its mixture of private and public enterprise, but within rather broad limits allows the forces of demand and supply to interact in such a way as to reconcile consumer sovereignty, the profit motive and public welfare. Fourth, and both consistent with and indispensable to each of the foregoing, is a relatively free collective bargaining system. As will be seen later no such system can be completely autonomous if it is to operate consistent with broader public priorities and programs, but it must be sufficiently independent to be a meaningful exercise to the parties involved. Fifth and finally, and again an integral part of the rest of the hierarchy, is an independent trade union movement. Such a movement is essential not only to countervail the power of employers over their employees but as part of the totality of a democratic pluralistic society.

Although these biases may lead the reader to suspect a rather critical judgement of what has been taking place in Western European industrial relations over the past decade, this has proven to be less the case than the author had anticipated. Obviously, however, this is a matter for the reader to decide, something he or she may be able to begin to do more effectively after grasping the scope and perusing the outline of this volume.

As for the scope of the volume, suffice it to point out for the moment what Western Europe embraces for present purposes. Besides Britain it includes the major continental countries of France, West Germany and Italy. It also covers Austria, Belgium and the Netherlands and the Scandinavian countries of Denmark, Norway, and Sweden. Greece, Portugal and Spain have been left out because they still lack some of the basic prerequisites of the aforementioned hierarchy of values and institutions. Other countries such as Ireland, Luxembourg and Switzerland have been ignored, largely because of their lack of influence and/or size.

OUTLINE OF THE VOLUME

This study begins with an attempt to define the meaning of the term industrial democracy and to explain the rationale behind the renewed drive for it. This is followed by an effort to capture the essence of some of the major differences between the North American and Western European industrial relations systems, while not losing sight of the variations which exist within each of these two separate systems. Some of the latest developments in Western European collective bargaining are then highlighted so as not to leave the impression that collective bargaining has somehow receded into the background as other forms of industrial democracy have evolved. With these three chapters as background, several chapters are then devoted to the growing influence of unions and workers at various levels in the overall socio-economic-political decision-making process. The chapters in question have titles which tend to speak for themselves: "Organized Labour and National Economic and Social Policy Formulation", "Joint or Tripartite Administration of Selected Public Programs", "Worker Representation on Company Boards", and "Works Councils". One composite chapter then deals with a variety of related topics including worker asset and capital formation plans; shop-floor democracy and the quality of working life; information and confidentiality; education and training; the multinational-corporation complication; and industrial democracy in the public service. Dealt with next are the prospective implications for both labour and management if industrial democracy in Western Europe continues to run its present course. Before the "Summary and Conclusion" there is a chapter on the "Implications and Relevance for North America".

Chapter 2

INDUSTRIAL DEMOCRACY:
ITS MEANING AND RATIONALE

Industrial democracy means so many different things to so many different people that one has to be hesitant about using the term. In one of its potentially most vague forms industrial democracy may be defined as any means by which unions and/or workers influence management decision-making at the enterprise level. From a more radical point of view industrial democracy may be viewed as the logical extension of political democracy, and thus the next natural step in the evolution of democratic forms of decision-making at all levels of the socio-economic-political system. This is doubtless what is implied by such goals as the total democratization of decision-making throughout society.

One distinction which should be made at the outset is the difference between industrial democracy and economic democracy. As used to date the former embraces various degrees of union and worker involvement in decision-making, while the latter is restricted to ways and means by which workers may share in the equity or ownership of enterprises. Little will be said about the latter until Chapter 9, which among other things deals with worker asset and capital formation plans. For the moment it will suffice to note that while such plans appear to be primarily designed to redistribute wealth in the form of share capital, this in itself could in time have a major impact upon corporate decision-making. Conversely, increasing worker participation in the strategic economic decision-making of enterprise through various forms of industrial democracy may well stimulate the demand for more economic democracy. This could well come about as employees come to appreciate the role of retained earnings as a major component in corporate growth.

Another point to be stressed at the beginning is that some forms of industrial democracy are becoming ever more contentious matters as it becomes more apparent that the underlying issue is that of power, which in Western Europe is intimately linked with class. As long as various types of industrial democracy do not encroach upon the basic rights and prerogatives of employers they do not provoke that much controversy. When industrial democracy in its more advanced state begins to impinge increasingly directly and frontally on management's position, there is bound to be a more open debate and test of strength.

One manifestation of this struggle over power is to be found in the terminology used by labour and management. Vague as it may be, most unions seem to prefer the term *industrial democracy*, if only because it implies more influence if not control. Trade unionists who aspire to take over completely from present-day management reject such phrases as *industrial democracy* in favour of those of *workers' control* and *self-management*. By contrast, employers usually choose to use the expressions *participative management* or at most *workers' participation* because they only tend to suggest limited consultative arrangements — thus leaving management free in the final analysis to manage as it sees fit in its own best judgement.

COLLECTIVE BARGAINING AND INDUSTRIAL DEMOCRACY: THE NORTH AMERICAN MODEL

North Americans still tend to view collective bargaining as the ultimate in industrial democracy. Given the way in which collective bargaining has evolved in North America, there is much to be said for this viewpoint. Nonetheless, it does tend to downplay at least two major considerations. The first of these lies in the fact that the majority of the North American labour force is not covered by collective bargaining. A second consideration is that political action is a more important ancillary activity of unions in North America than many foreign observers are prepared to acknowledge or realize.

These qualifications aside, there is no doubt that the vast majority of organized workers in North America are well served by their unions through collective bargaining when it comes to their conditions and terms of employment. Collective agreements are comprehensive and elaborate in North America. They are detailed and lengthy and are gradually being expanded to cover more and more issues. For the most part employers enjoy only residual rights in the form of past custom and practice in those areas not dealt with under a collective agreement. As for enforcement of agreements, organized labour in North America has its base at the plant or union hiring-hall level where its power is concentrated. To ensure that agreements are respected they usually have sophisticated grievance and arbitration machinery at their disposal.

Admittedly and at best, North American collective bargaining only deals with employee-employer relations at the industry, company or plant level. This is one of the reasons why neither the American nor the Canadian labour movements can rely solely on collective bargaining. It would be most unrealistic for them not to be involved in politics. They have to take political action not only to ensure a favourable legislative framework for their bargaining activities, but to foster sympathetic government intervention in major disputes. In addition, they must also look to government for the maintenance of a healthy economy and for the promotion of minimum labour standards and other forms of social security more readily provided by the state.

Taking into consideration every form of union and worker involvement in pertinent decision-making in North America there is no doubt that collective bargaining is the centrepiece and mainstay of the influences they are able to exercise. Were it not for the way in which North American unions are organized at all levels, down to and including the plant level, and for the comparative comprehensiveness of North American collective agreements, there might be no comparison between this type of industrial democracy and some of the variations on it which are to be found in Western Europe. So far North American workers have been relatively well served by their system of industrial democracy. Their comparative position in this respect could well be slipping, however, as Western European unions supplement their collective bargaining and political activities with a number of other means of influencing decision-making at all levels of society.

BEYOND COLLECTIVE BARGAINING: THE WESTERN EUROPEAN EXPERIENCE

Although some of the developments mentioned in this section are also to be found in limited degrees in North America, it is fair to state that for the most part they have made much more headway in Western Europe. This distinction is doubtless to be explained in part by the differing nature of the collective bargaining systems involved, something which will be discussed at length in the next chapter. For the moment it is sufficient to note that because collective bargaining in Western Europe has tended to be more national or regional in character, other mechanisms were bound to emerge to serve the more parochial company and plant level concerns of workers. This point does not begin to explain everything that follows, but it does help one to understand some of the more unique features of industrial democracy in Western Europe.

First of all it must be recognized that industrial democracy or workers' participation can take either direct or indirect forms. The former entails concepts in which workers themselves are directly involved, such as job enlargement, job enrichment, job rotation and semi-autonomous work groups. Concepts such as these are discussed later in Chapter 9 under the heading "Shop-Floor Democracy and the Quality of Working Life". Indirect forms of industrial democracy or workers' participation do not involve workers directly, but rather through their representatives whether they be stewards, trustmen or other union officials, members of works councils, or worker representatives on company boards.

Beyond collective bargaining as such, and varying forms and types of political action, Western European unions and workers have become involved in a host of bodies where they can influence decision-making at all levels of the economy and society. Each of these areas will be the subject of a later chapter or section. Nonetheless they need to be mentioned at this point to indicate how potent a voice they could provide organized labour if combined effectively all together in one system.

The labour movement in several Western European countries is well represented in national economic and social consultative bodies which sometimes have a great deal of influence on overall government policy formulation. Organized labour in a few countries is not only well represented on other types of consultative bodies — especially in the social security field — but also has a major say in the actual administration and operation of some public programs of major concern to workers. The ground is being laid in more and more countries for one version or another of West Germany's so-called codetermination. This is the system which provides for varying proportions of union and worker representatives on the supervisory board of the two-tier company board structures which prevail in that country. Below this level many countries in Western Europe have works councils with differing employee-employer compositions and varying degrees of worker rights in relation to information, consultation and codecision-making.

There are no significant examples of worker control or self-management in Western Europe, although a number of cooperatives and a few enterprises which have been taken over by their workers do apparently operate on this basis. The only country with extensive experience in this form of management is Yugoslavia, which has been left out of this survey because it does not fit into the liberal-democratic-enterprise framework which is still the hallmark of the other countries included. This is not to deny that there may be much to learn from the Yugoslavian experience. What there is to learn, however, must be seen in the light of the overall nature of the society involved — a task which goes far beyond the scope of this analysis.

The problem with each of the other forms of industrial democracy mentioned above is to try to ascertain what they have led to in practice. Only then can one begin to assess whether they have garnered Western European unions and workers any more advances than their North American counterparts under straightforward collective bargaining. This is hardly the only test of the relative worth of these various forms of industrial democracy, but it is one that should not be ignored as interest in these concepts spreads.

Still another distinction which must be drawn is that between decision-making and decision-taking. This is not necessarily just a play on words when applied to a collective bargaining process or to other forms of industrial democracy. Very often the groundwork is laid and the preparations are made for decisions in forums other than where they are actually taken. In and of itself this fact of decision-making life is not to be criticized or condemned, unless it is part of a deliberate charade designed to belittle and bypass the formal procedures in question. It is important to be aware of this possibility in trying to appreciate the efficacy of any type of industrial democracy.

THE GROWING INTEREST IN INDUSTRIAL DEMOCRACY

Many explanations have been offered for the growing interest in new forms of industrial democracy. Among the more popular of these explanations is that emphasizing purported changes in the attitude of workers towards work. This is usually attributed to rising educational levels. Yet changes in the quality of education may be even more significant than changes in its quantity. This is due in part to the acquisition of relatively more knowledge outside the formal school system through life itself, the media and politics. Educational systems themselves have become more democratic and open, and less formal and structured. Flexible classroom arrangements, group learning and variable curricula have become commonplace. Regardless of the other consequences of these changes, one result has been a more participative approach to learning. Once acquired, participative habits are not easily sublimated, either at the plant or office door.

Another set of factors, allegedly contributing to a different attitude towards work, concerns the hierarchy of needs which apparently motivates workers. Supposedly having satisfied much of their need for wages and salaries to pay for food, clothing and shelter it is argued that workers no longer just look upon their jobs as a means to provide them with a livelihood. Instead they not only expect to derive a good income from their employment but to be able to realize through work some of man's higher order needs, ranging from creativity to self-esteem.

Far from meeting these higher order needs a strong case can be made that many jobs serve to frustrate them. Modern technology depends on economies of scale, necessitating large organizations with their attendant bureaucratization and depersonalization. Added to this are many jobs which impose a degree of monotony and/or repetition well below the mentality and potential skill levels of those expected to perform them. Under circumstances such as these it is quite conceivable that after a certain point more money will not compensate for the inherent frustrations involved.

The problem with this type of analysis is that it is hard to document or prove. Certainly there are numerous signs of disenchantment among the work forces of many countries. Manifestations of discontent range from some of the collective demonstrations and protests mentioned earlier to high rates of absenteeism, low morale and reduced productivity. These represent signs of alienation to the behaviouralist which take negative forms in the absence of more constructive outlets. Presumably various types of industrial democracy might provide such outlets, although there is precious little sign of any rank and file push for such measures.

Lending credence to the alienation school is the fact that younger workers in particular seem more prone to opt for the growing alternatives to work which are now available. Although unemployment insurance and other income maintenance standards are hardly generous, they increasingly tend to approach the minimum levels of pay which are offered for many unskilled jobs. If the work involved is anything but edifying and the extra income to be earned from that work is only marginally above state assistance of one kind or another, it is hardly surprising that some individuals should prefer subsidized idleness.

That something is amiss about the work ethic is also suggested by the lengths to which many managements are willing to go on their own initiative to make work more attractive. Especially when plagued by increased turnover due to high resignation rates, employers are driven to pay higher wages and salaries and to do everything else they can to provide their employees with greater job satisfaction. Thus, when it comes to efforts to improve the quality of working life at the shop floor level, the lead has in the past, at least, been frequently taken by management.

In contrast, union interest in industrial democracy usually focuses on its more indirect forms, such as codetermination or works councils. More often than not union demands in this area are part of a broader commitment to the democratization of decision-making at all levels of society. This ideological commitment may appear on the surface to represent little more than a grasp for more power, but in some union quarters at least there is a deep underlying political objective that should not be minimized.

A more pragmatic reason for unions and workers demanding broader forms of industrial democracy grows out of the apparent limitations of collective bargaining in a number of areas and respects. Aside from the lack of coverage and limited scope of collective bargaining in many countries, there is the non-continuous and sporadic nature of the process and its ultimate dependence on the power relationship between the parties. This power equation may vary with everything from the nature of the issue involved to the state of the economy. On some issues, such as plant closures and other forms of industrial conversions, the collective bargaining process often seems quite inadequate to cope with the situation. Failure to respond effectively to these kinds of problems brings out significant deficiencies in many existing negotiating procedures.

All too frequently in the past, for example, unions and workers have had to negotiate agreements in the absence of highly pertinent information which has been deliberately withheld from them. This may not be a major problem when it comes to concessions over pay and benefits, but it can make a critical difference if a large reduction in staff or plant shutdown is in the offing. In all too many cases, collective bargaining is made to appear as a reactive process responding to crises after it is too late to do anything but accept a fait accompli and offer a modest amount of assistance and consolation to those adversely affected by the change in question. It takes only a few instances such as these to drive some trade unionists to demand access to the bodies responsible for initiating and introducing such changes. Their numbers tend to swell when job insecurity increases because of high unemployment, as has been the case for a few years now in several of the countries covered by this study. The fact that these difficulties have plagued countries governed by parties sympathetic to labour, as well as other countries, has further swelled the ranks of union representatives favouring new forms of industrial democracy. It now appears that neither collective bargaining nor political action, let alone both together, are enough to control such disruptive events.

Not to be neglected in any catalogue of the explanations for the rising interest in various forms of industrial democracy is the role played by intellectuals and international agencies. On the intellectual front the behaviouralists and the political scientists tend to be the most active in the campaign for industrial democracy. They and other like-minded intellectuals form the intelligentsia behind the real wielders of power who are promoting this cause. Many of the latter in turn are to be found in a variety of international agencies, ranging from the International Labour Organization (ILO) to the Organization for Economic Cooperation and Development (OECD). Although bodies such as the ILO and the OECD only publish reports and sponsor conferences and seminars on industrial democracy, these activities in themselves foster more interest in the subject. By far the most important international body behind the push for industrial democracy is the European Economic Community (EEC). As will be seen in later chapters it has been responsible for promulgating two major proposals on company reform which have done much to promote the drive for codetermination and other forms of industrial democracy throughout Western Europe. Some of the reasons for this EEC thrust are dealt with in the last section of this chapter.

Last but not least of the reasons for more interest in industrial democracy is the role of the media. If only by playing up the more militant and sensational aspects of labour relations, such as the seizures by workers of plants when threatened by mass layoffs, the media have added to the feeling of uneasiness about the present system. This in itself has played into the hands of those who favour new forms of industrial democracy by dramatizing the shortcomings of the present one.

UNION AMBIVALENCE

Lest one leave the impression that all trade unionists in Western Europe favour more industrial democracy, it should be made clear that there is still a lot of ambivalence among their ranks. This is particularly true when it comes to the issue of union and worker representation on company boards, but it also applies in other areas as well.

As for codetermination, some union skeptics have rather pragmatic reasons for doubts, while others have more ideological and philosophical misgivings and reservations. The pragmatic skeptics tend to be rather North American in their orientation, in that they worry about conflicts of interest and the two-hat dilemma. Rather than becoming involved in making management decisions which might run contrary to their members' interests they prefer to retain the unfettered right to challenge such decisions. They believe that they would compromise that right by sitting on management decision-making bodies in any capacity.

While sharing this concern some trade unionists are prepared to sit on management decision-making bodies to gain information and insight and to ensure that the workers' point of view is considered. They would still consider themselves trade unionists first and accordingly would reserve the right to challenge the decisions arrived at in any way they could should they run counter to their members' interests. This is obviously the most troublesome group of trade unionists for a company to contemplate or live with on its board.

Most trade unionists on the far left remain strongly opposed to any form of codetermination, on the grounds that it all too easily leads to union and worker cooptation and integration. Dedicated as they are to a new socio-economic-political order they are naturally leery of any step which might strengthen the present system or even lessen criticism of it. Nothing less than nationalization and workers' control or self-management will satisfy this group of unionists, although it remains to be seen what would happen if they or their allies actually gained political power. In the meantime at least, they can hardly afford to countenance any schemes which could reduce worker militancy and, thus, the driving force behind their desire for radical change.

The latter provisos raise what may turn out to be the most fundamental question of all for trade unionists who believe in democratizing all levels of decision-making in society. The basic issue then becomes that of power and responsibility. It is clearly debatable how much power unions can acquire without assuming commensurate responsibility. If unions choose to become fully involved in every possible decision-making body it is questionable how much real freedom of action they can retain. There is no easy or ready answer to this dilemma, as will be brought out in a later chapter on ''Industrial Democracy and the Future of Labour and Management''.

Although union ambivalence about codetermination in particular remains prevalent in most countries of Western Europe it is important to note that there has been a steady swing towards a more favourable reaction over the past few years. In country after country the middle ground of trade union opinion has been shifting persistently in the direction of a more positive attitude toward this form of industrial democracy as well as most of the others. This shift or swing in opinion in most cases is based on certain minimal conditions for union and worker participation in such ventures, which will be brought out in later chapters.

EMPLOYER CONCERNS

As will become increasingly apparent as this study proceeds employer attitudes towards industrial democracy depend very much on the form which it takes. As already suggested, employers tend to view some forms of workers' participation quite positively, as long as they pose no serious threats to their right to manage. On their own initiative many firms have been promoting more participative styles of management involving more decentralization, less close supervision, more on-the-job responsibility, and so on. Employer resistance at this level of industrial democracy may only arise when the economic costs threaten to outweigh the benefits — as can quite conceivably happen when expensive new equipment is required to facilitate semi-autonomous work groups and the like.

Management opinion begins to divide on higher degrees of industrial democracy, depending in large measure on the experience which they have had. As a generalization it is probably safe to say that the less exposed an employer has been to any form of industrial democracy, the more he or she fears it. This is not just fear of the unknown. It involves much more than that. Flexibility and freedom of management can be a decisive variable in the success of any enterprise. Consequently any threat to management's flexibility and freedom is bound to be viewed with some trepidation. Such fears are invariably heightened when outside union officials, as well as a company's own workers, are likely to be involved in any new industrial democracy ventures.

As for those who have lived with various forms of industrial democracy, it is remarkable how accustomed they can become to just about anything. It is in this sense that management's capacity to adjust is often quite astounding. Employers have learned to live with many forms of industrial democracy, including collective bargaining itself in some pretty advanced and aggressive forms. Currently the most disputed form of industrial democracy is undoubtedly codetermination at the corporate board level. Although a considerable body of employer opinion is now prepared to live with minority union and worker representation on supervisory-type company boards, the vast majority of firms remain unalterably opposed to parity of union and worker and shareholder representation. It is at this point that managers can become as ideological and philosophical in their orientation and thinking as their union counterparts. In management's view parity of representation does not just threaten its capacity to manage efficiently and productively, but ultimately the very nature of the enterprise or market system itself. At the very least, employers express grave misgivings and reservations about the effect of parity codetermination on the autonomy of the social partners — to use Western European phraseology — in the collective bargaining arena. How, they wonder, can organized labour be represented on both sides of the bargaining table without compromising its position and the very integrity of the negotiating process itself? Some managers vigorously and vociferously extend the threat posed by advanced forms of industrial democracy to the survival of a pluralistic and therefore democratic and free society. That these are not just idle debating points or extravagant rhetoric will again be brought out in the later chapter on "Industrial Democracy and the Future of Labour and Management".

GOVERNMENT INTEREST

Given the widely divergent views which exist among and between unions and employers about most forms of industrial democracy, it is not surprising that this is yet another critical area of public policy where government has the decisive voice. On the whole this study will tend to show that Western European governments have been using their power to introduce more and more forms of industrial democracy with majority union backing and majority, if not total, employer resistance. It is interesting to explore the reason for this trend which may lie deeper than simple crass political considerations. Even if they may be the overriding factors in the long run — as a section in the next chapter will suggest — there is an intellectual case to be made for more industrial democracy of all kinds which has some appeal.

This case is made within the Commission of the EEC as well as in a number of Western European capitals. Within the EEC itself, it goes beyond the so-called democratic imperative which holds that those affected by decisions made by economic and social institutions must have a meaningful voice in them. Beyond this consideration, both EEC and individual government initiatives in the field of industrial democracy are based on the notion that Western Europe could be in serious trouble in the not-too-distant future because of its lack of basic resources and raw materials — especially in terms of sources of energy. Because of this deficiency, Western Europe must depend for its well-being on its ability to manufacture and transform goods for the world market. This market is becoming increasingly competitive as countries with lower wages catch up technologically. Western Europe must somehow stay ahead technologically to offset its higher wage levels. To do this it must harness all the human ingenuity it can and induce high savings in order to finance heavy investment.

As for harnessing human ingenuity it is argued that this cannot possibly take place within industrial relations systems which are prone to strikes and lockouts and other forms of industrial conflict, let alone class conflict and polarization. Rather, this can only happen within a consensual model such as West Germany's, where organized labour is probably just about as well represented in all levels of decision-making as in any other Western European country. The fact that much of the Common Market's proposed company legislation is based on modified versions of German codetermination tends to bear out this interpretation of why the EEC and more of its member states are now so eager to move in this direction.

Turning to the related savings-investment challenge the first point to be made is that the wages-fund theory is dead. As originally or at least popularly interpreted, this was the theory that advocated that workers take less pay now in return for better prospects later on. By paying out less in wages, firms would be able to generate more funds for investment, thereby enhancing their capacity to pay more in the future. The problem with this theory was and is that labour received no guarantee of any future pay-off, while shareholders often secured larger short- and long-run returns. Today, if workers are to be persuaded to moderate their wage and salary claims for the sake of more investment in plant and equipment, they may have to be offered a share in the proceeds. This is why the next big push for industrial democracy in Western Europe could come in the form of the worker asset or capital formation plans that are discussed in Chapter 9.

THE PROCESS AND THE RESULTS

However defined, industrial democracy at the enterprise level involves the challenge of democratizing or making more participative structures which have in the past been largely authoritarian and hierarchical in nature. In its most idealistic and utopian form industrial democracy raises the question of whether constitutional government can be applied to industry and commerce as well as society at large in the political sphere. To varying extents this has already occurred, if only through the collective bargaining process.

One has to query how far this and other related processes of industrial democracy can be pursued. It is one thing to control the abuses of capital in relation to labour; it is another to involve workers in differing forms of codecision-making. But it is quite another world when this leads to management by consensus or consent or even to self-management, whatever the latter means. That there is such a spectrum of possibilities — at least up to, if not including, the latter — will become apparent as this volume proceeds.

It is critical, in the meantime, to point out that it is hard to assess the results of all these developments unless one is something of an ideologue at either end of the spectrum of viewpoints which exists on these concepts. Some of the true believers in industrial democracy are almost religious in their convictions. The processes are as important as the results. The hard-nosed skeptics, in contrast, are sometimes so opposed to the process that they cannot bring themselves to look at the results.

Those in between with a more pragmatic orientation are usually interested in the impact of industrial democracy on a combination of economic efficiency and job satisfaction. They tend to be inclined to examine different forms and types of industrial democracy in the light of these criteria. If the mechanism in question enhances both efficiency and satisfaction there is no doubt about its desirability. This is also the case if it improves one without detracting from the other. The problem arises where tradeoffs are involved.

Such tradeoffs normally involve some sacrifice of economic efficiency in return for more job satisfaction. The trend is clearly towards the acceptance of more risks in this respect, if only because society is now placing more emphasis on the human being as distinct from the productive process. Yet there must be limits to such a preference, unless one is willing to forego more growth than most people appear to want to — if one is to judge by their desire for material goods and services.

Chapter 3

INDUSTRIAL RELATIONS IN NORTH AMERICA AND WESTERN EUROPE:
SOME BASIC CONTRASTS

Before proceeding further it is essential to clarify some of the key differences between industrial relations in North America and Western Europe. It is also necessary to highlight some of the major distinctions within each of these two sets of industrial relations systems.

INDUSTRIAL RELATIONS IN NORTH AMERICA AND WESTERN EUROPE

The major differences between North American and Western European industrial relations can most conveniently be brought out under four headings: the environment, the parties of interest, interaction processes, and results.

The Environment

There are many facets of the general socio-economic-political environment which affect the nature of an industrial relations system. North America and Western Europe outwardly share much in common in this overall sense. Despite some differences in interpretation which are brought out below, both still extol fundamental Western values relating to the maintenance of as much individual freedom as possible. Consistent with these values, both also govern themselves in accordance with liberal-democratic principles. The mixed-free-enterprise or modified-capitalist economic system still prevails in both systems, although more so in North America than in much of Western Europe.

North America, and the United States in particular, appears to have more faith in the enterprise system than seems to be true of many parts of Western Europe. Aside from West Germany, which in some ways is now more American than the United States, much of Western Europe is beset by a great deal of soul-searching about everything pertaining to the capitalist system. In part, as will be noted more forcefully shortly, this distinction doubtless reflects North America's greater tolerance for abuses arising under this system. One possible, although highly debatable, ramification of this distinction relates to the work ethic. Again, with some noteworthy exceptions in Western Europe, it can be argued, but hardly proven, that the work ethic may be in less trouble in North America. The explanation for the difference in this case may simply lie in the remnants of the frontier mentality that still prevails in much of North America.

Perhaps the best way to characterize these basic underlying distinctions is in terms of the degrees of individualism and collectivism accepted and embodied in the two systems. North America still tends to epitomize individualism in the sense of the relatively unrestrained pursuit of self interest, on the assumption and in the belief that this approach will in the end ensure the fastest overall pace of economic progress. This fundamental set of premises permeates North American society to the point that its economic system might best be described as capitalism with a vengeance. Especially as practiced in the United States, this form of capitalism has paid off handsomely in terms of such broad economic measures as its gross national product. But the same system has produced gross disparities of income, inadequate basic standards of health care and other forms of social security, and many other manifestations of an almost brutal non-caring insensitive society.

In contrast to North America's greater reliance on individualism, Western Europe puts more faith in collectivism, which is not necessarily to be confused, let alone equated, with communism or socialism. Even in their educational systems many Western European countries play down self-assertion in favour of group endeavours. In some countries this deemphasis of one of the basic ingredients of capitalism doubtless helps to explain why it has not generated that much production and wealth for its people. Yet this may be more than offset by the fact that some of these same countries are more prone to look after their disadvantaged and downtrodden. This reflects the higher value they place on the common good and social justice.

Until a few years ago the country which seemed to combine the best of these two systems was Sweden which practiced capitalism with a conscience, as distinct from the United States' version which might be described as capitalism with a vengeance. Swedish business was permitted to pursue its self-interest in the form of higher profits, and in the process helped generate a rapidly rising national income. A large part of the proceeds was then channeled into one of the world's most efficient, equitable and generous social security systems. Although Sweden thus seemed to have the best of both worlds something has since gone wrong in the country. Not satisfied with one of the highest standards of living in the world, the Swedish people began to make demands of their system, which far outstripped its capacity to satisfy them. The country is now plagued by both economic and political uncertainty to the point where it is hazardous to attempt to project what may happen next.

Returning to some of the overall contrasts between North America and Western Europe there is still another facet of the difference between the two that is extremely hard to document. Although the energy crisis, Vietnam and Watergate have all shaken the confidence of the United States, and mismanagement of its economy and the Quebec crisis have had a similar effect in Canada, North America remains both an optimistic and opportunistic continent. Reflecting its war torn history and more current preoccupation with such concerns as its heavy dependence on foreign sources of energy, most of Western Europe is characterized by a more pessimistic and security-conscious mood.

Growing out of some of the foregoing contrasts is a more marked distinction between North America and Western Europe which is to be found in the political sphere. While majority government is the norm in North America, this is anything but the case in Western Europe. Most countries in Western Europe have minority governments so coalition, compromise and consensual politics are the order of the day. In many countries this has led to a very fluid and unstable situation in which a small shift in votes can lead to marked change in public policies either to the left or to the right. While the long-run trend is clearly to the left, the pendulum does tend to swing back to the right periodically but not sharply.

Occasional checks on the underlying political shift to the left are to be found more in the northern than the southern countries of Western Europe. Recent examples of this phenomenon emerged in Germany and Sweden. In several other countries, most notably France and Italy, it is now largely a question of how far and fast they are going to move to the left. The emergence of Eurocommunism as a more respectable political force is noteworthy in this respect. Having proclaimed their willingness, whether in or out of office, to abide by the democratic will of the people and having declared their intention not to be blind adherents of the Russian brand of communism, the Eurocommunists are now in a better position to move towards a grand alliance with the more centre left social democratic parties. As a result of this astute political maneuvering by the Eurocommunists — as questionable as it may or may not be — they could soon form part of the government in both France and Italy. Where this could eventually lead is anyone's guess.

All of this makes politics a very active and pervasive element in virtually all areas of life in Western Europe. As a result the industrial relations process tends to be highly politicized with both labour and management depending on their political allies much more heavily than is the case in North America. This tends to work to the advantage of unions more than the employers since they obviously represent more votes. Regardless of their political persuasion this makes all governments in Western Europe more receptive to union demands. Because of their frequent minority status, however, they cannot be too responsive to any one group. This same status is what inclines most governments in Western Europe to engage in a great deal of consultation with all concerned before proceeding with any new legislative initiatives or policy innovations.

As indicated earlier government by coalition, compromise and consensus is much more common in Western Europe than North America. Whether by formal or informal means a much greater attempt is made in Western Europe to obtain the acceptance, or at least the acquiescence, of all major elements likely to be affected by new government undertakings. This does not always work out, as employer spokesmen in many countries now bear witness. Reflecting the persistent leftward shift of public policies all over Western Europe, these spokesmen insist that at best they are fighting a defensive and losing rearguard action against this trend. This growing feeling of despair applies to the field of labour law as well as many other related areas.

The role of law in industrial relations is much different in North America than in Western Europe. Both the United States and Canada rely on complex statutory frameworks to regulate virtually every facet of labour-management relations. There are protracted certification procedures to ensure that legitimate unions with majority employee support are granted exclusive bargaining rights within appropriate bargaining units. There are also a host of unfair labour practices precluding both unions and employers from engaging in certain types of activities and conduct, such as illegal strikes or lockouts. To administer and enforce the detailed laws pertaining to industrial relations there are quasi-judicial tribunals known as labour relations boards which, despite the best of original intentions, have become increasingly formal and legalistic in their procedures.

All this legal paraphernalia is almost unknown in Western Europe, where labour law tends to play a quite different role. Although legislation calling for a peace obligation during the life of a collective agreement is quite common in Western Europe — as in most of Canada, but not the United States — and a variety of labour courts and other types of tribunals have been put in place to settle individual rights disputes arising under applicable agreements and statutes, this tends to be the limit of legislative regulation of the collective bargaining process. Unions have the lawful right to exist and to take effective industrial action, and thereafter it is more or less left up to labour and management to resolve their differences as best they can.

Labour legislation in Western Europe plays a much greater role in the establishment of minimum standards of employment and social security than is the case in North America. Western Europe is much more prone than North America to use minimum labour standards legislation, not only to place a floor under wage and other forms of labour competition but to provide more generous standards of employment in keeping with those enjoyed by organized workers. It is quite common in Western Europe for the minimum standards embodied in national and regional negotiations to be extended to unorganized as well as organized firms within the industries involved.

Having made these basic distinctions in terms of the application of law in the two systems, it must be added that Western Europe is now in the throes of introducing much more statutory regulation of the mechanisms for industrial democracy which complement the collective bargaining process and minimum labour standards. Some countries, such as Austria and Germany, have a long history of legislation pertaining to codetermination and works councils. Their statutes in these areas are becoming more complex and elaborate, while other Western European countries are now moving in the same general direction. Western European laws in these areas could well become as complicated and pervasive as those of North America in its more narrowly defined sphere of collective bargaining.

Union uneasiness in Western Europe about their place at the enterprise or plant level has now led them to successfully insist on more statutory recognition of their position and role at these levels. Even more markedly parallel legislation to that found in North America has emerged in a few countries, such as Britain and Sweden, where unions have again successfully insisted on a number of new statutory provisions strengthening their legal status within the total industrial relations system.

The Parties of Interest

There are many parties of interest in the industrial relations system besides labour and management. Most notable among the other parties of interest are governments and the public at large. For present purposes it will suffice to deal only with the major differences between unions and employers in North America and Western Europe.

Organizationally and structurally there are many differences between North American and Western European unions. North American unions are organized with many overlapping jurisdictions by industry and craft or trade. Industrial unions predominate in secondary manufacturing, the public service and the resource sector, while craft or trade unions continue to maintain their strength in the construction industry and in a few other cases. Whether industrial or craft or trade in scope, all North American unions are relatively well organized from the top down to the job, office or shop floor level. Full time business agents or international representatives are available on a fairly extensive basis to aid local union officers in the servicing of the membership. Perhaps the weakest point in the North American labour movement is to be found at the national federation level. Neither the AFL-CIO nor its Canadian counterpart, the Canadian Labour Congress (CLC), has very much power. Periodically they do have considerable influence as political lobbies, but that is the most meaningful role which they have played to date.

With the exception of Britain, West Germany, Sweden and a few other countries, Western European trade unions remain divided along ideological, philosophical and religious lines. Although these divisions are gradually giving way to a more unified labour movement in some countries, it is still common to have two or three competing industrial unions in every sector of the economy. Equally striking and more universal in Western Europe is the comparative weakness of unions at the job, office or plant level. Although unions in Sweden and a few other countries have effective local unions, these do not form the bases of the labour movement as they do in North America. In contrast, the central federations of labour have much more influence than their opposite numbers in North America. Even when there are competing national labour centres, they are regularly consulted by government and are a major force to be reckoned with in national policy formulation.

Particularly confusing to the North American observer are the number of different types of representatives which exist at the work level to serve employee interests in some European countries. This seemingly undue duplication grows out of the overlapping jurisdictions of collective bargaining and other forms of industrial democracy at this level in these countries. To illustrate one need only cite the case of France which like

Italy represents the most extreme example of this kind of duplication. In France, since 1936, there have been employee delegates to handle individual grievances arising under pertinent laws and national or regional collective agreements. In 1945, works councillors were added to handle the problems dealt with by the work councils discussed in a later chapter. Finally, in 1968, union delegates gained formal status as such as part of the settlement of the crisis that swept the country in that year. Their job is to handle union business at their level, which means there are many of them because of the rival unions present in most enterprises and plants.

Although the situation is not as confusing in most other Western European countries it could be moving in this direction, if only because special health and safety representatives are now being introduced by law or collective agreement in many of these countries. Together with the union stewards or trustmen and the almost universal works councillors, this means that many Western European countries have at least three types of employee representatives at the works level. As confusing as this situation may appear, it is often lessened by the fact that the same individuals may occupy more than one position. Moreover, as unions become more active and assertive at the enterprise or plant level, they tend to exercise a coordinating influence over all those involved.

Western European unions tend to be much more ideological and political in their orientation than their North American counterparts. While many of the leading industrial unions in North America are actively involved in pursuing reform through political action, the scope for such reform activities — even among the most progressive of these unions — tends to be limited relative to the Western European situation. Even where unions are formally neutral or non-aligned in politics — as in the case of the German Confederation of Labour (DGB) in West Germany — they are very active politically. In many countries of Western Europe the unions are divided along the same lines as the political parties they support. Thus there are often Catholic, Communist and Social Democratic alliances among the political parties and unions in question. The fact that the far left pursues its strong ideological connections with such zeal forces the more moderate centrist groups to become equally active. As a result, whether just reform or revolution is the ultimate goal, Western European unions and their allies are much more ideologically inclined and politically oriented than are their North American counterparts.

Another way of putting the distinction between North American and

Western European unions is as follows. North American unions are basically job conscious organizations and they thus concentrate on improving their members' lot in terms of wages and working conditions at the level of the individual employer or employers. Given their broader orientation Western European unions have traditionally devoted most of their attention to industry-wide or national priorities. Just as Western European unions are now focussing more of their efforts at the work level, so North American unions are showing increasing interest in more global issues. In this sense there may be a gradual convergence taking place in their overall approaches and outlook.

On the employer side the differences are much less marked than on the union side. It may well be that North American management has a greater ideological commitment to capitalism, but this would be hard to prove. Their opposite numbers in Western Europe have had to learn to accommodate to governments which are less committed to capitalism. Being as pragmatic as their North American counterparts they have dropped some of the capitalist rhetoric while trying to retain as much of its substance as they can. This defensive rearguard action does not mean they are any less committed to the market system. Rather it implies that they have to wage a more sophisticated campaign to preserve what is left of it.

Because of the defensive rearguard nature of the posture they have felt forced to adopt in recent years, Western European employers have become increasingly formal, legalistic and even ritualistic in their strategies. In this sense they undoubtedly still have much to learn from North American employers, who have been driven to the same conclusion by the highly restrictive statutory frameworks within which they have had to operate for years. The results in both cases are often unfortunate, as more direct and open relations with organized labour can be much more productive. Employers and unions which choose to get along reasonably amicably under either system usually find ways to conduct their affairs in less formal, legalistic and ritualistic manners.

Because the collective bargaining process is more centralized, and because industrial relations and the entire socio-economic system is so much more politicized in Western Europe, employers there have had to build up more effective industry federations and national confederations than are to be found in North America. National and regional bargaining by industry has compelled companies to organize effective employer associations parallel to the arrangements on the union side. The need to represent broad employer and management interests at the national level before the government and in public forums has forced them to place an equal amount of emphasis on their national confederation or inter-industry bodies. Even so, much remains to be done by employers collectively in most Western European countries if they are to match the mounting influence and power of the union aggregations which now confront them, particularly in the political sphere.

Interaction Processes

Collective bargaining is much more central to the North American industrial relations system than to that of Western Europe. This is because North American unions have concluded to date that they can achieve far more through collective bargaining than they can through any of the alternatives now available to them. Although they do engage in a limited range of political action they have never thought of this approach as beginning to compete with that of collective bargaining in terms of its payoff. Nor, as already underscored, have they paid any significant heed to forms of industrial democracy other than collective bargaining.

Meanwhile, in Western Europe a variety of current and historical factors combine to explain why unions do not place as much reliance on collective bargaining, even though it is still the most crucial instrument in terms of the total array of forces they have at their disposal to improve the lot of their members. One critical point that has to be borne in mind relates to what may be described as a kind of macro-micro tradeoff in which many Western European unions are engaged, whether formally or otherwise. In return for a more influential voice at the macro level in national socio-economic policy formulation, these unions have apparently been prepared to moderate and restrain their demands at the micro level in collective bargaining. The full dimensions of this tradeoff will become more apparent in the following two chapters. The point to be stressed for the moment is that there is a clear-cut tradeoff involved which is the major current reason why many unions in Western Europe are prepared to place relatively less reliance on collective bargaining in and of itself.

Another aspect of most Western European industrial relations systems which is to be emphasized is that it takes place on at least two levels. This is why it is so common to hear of Western Europe's dual level of bargaining. For the most part unions as such confine their collective bargaining activities to national and regional level negotiations which establish minimum standards of pay and certain other limited terms and conditions of employment. Aside from a trend within these national and regional negotiations to cover a widening range of employment conditions, it is also increasingly common for them to specify the procedures under which lower levels of bargaining are to take place. Although some company level bargaining has emerged along more North American lines, this is still very much the exception rather than the rule. Instead it is customary to leave it to the other levels of bargaining to supplement the gains made and to fill in the gaps left by the negotiations at the national or regional level.

This other level of bargaining may take place at the company, plant or work level. It may involve union stewards as in Britain, works councillors as in West Germany, or workers' delegates as in Italy. There is little commonality to this lower level of dual bargaining, except for the fact that it plays an extremely important part in determining workers' actual pay and working conditions which often go well beyond those set out in national and regional agreements. This is why more and more unions are trying to take over the various instruments which now exist to bargain at these lower levels. Otherwise their members may continue to wonder what purpose their unions really serve, since their nationally or regionally negotiated rates are usually well below those they actually receive.

Grievance or rights disputes are also handled somewhat differently in Western Europe than in North America. In the latter these disputes are usually settled in accordance with grievance and arbitration procedures agreed to by the parties in their collective agreements. It is not so simple in Western Europe where the range of practices is again quite wide. In Britain failure by the parties to resolve such disputes means that they may end up in mediation, arbitration or industrial action. On the continent labour courts play a greater role in these matters, especially where there is a mandatory peace obligation during the life of a collective agreement. If a grievance or rights dispute cannot be resolved by the worker himself or his or her steward, works councillor, or worker's delegate, the worker may take the case before a labour court with or without union or other support. In any event the decision of the labour court is normally final and binding on all concerned.

As for outright industrial conflict, North America, and especially Canada, usually loses more time due to strikes and lockouts as a percentage of all time worked than all Western European countries except Italy. Strikes or lockouts in North America seldom involve more than one plant or one company or one industry at the most; but when they do occur they are often protracted if only because both sides tend to prepare for major struggles once their relationship shows signs of deteriorating to the point of open conflict. Western European strikes tend in contrast to be more global and political in nature. Although there are sometimes major confrontations at the industry, company or plant level, widespread demonstration and protest actions seem to be a more prevalent manifestation of industrial unrest.

Results

The differing results of the North American and Western European industrial relations systems can be summarized very briefly, as they should already be fairly apparent and will reappear again in one guise or another in later chapters. North American industrial relations feature detailed collective bargaining and contract administration by relatively well organized unions at the industry, company or plant level. While it is more difficult to generalize about Western Europe, its industrial relations tend to rely on broad union or inter-union industry framework bargaining at the national or regional level, supplemented by a wide variety of company and plant level arrangements which carry on where the framework negotiations leave off.

One result of these two separate approaches is that informal agreements and bargaining appear to be much more commonplace in Western Europe than North America. Although informal arrangements are far from unknown in North America, there is less need for them because collective agreements are so much more comprehensive. Employers in North America also tend to be more leery of such arrangements, lest they become precedents in future arbitration proceedings or subsequent rounds of negotiations. Lacking elaborate formal contracts within which to operate, Western European managers and workers are much more disposed to enter into informal understandings. The need is obviously present, and there is less reason to fear the results as they are unlikely to prove binding on either side in their later relations.

VARIATIONS WITHIN NORTH AMERICA

Before turning to the much more complicated variations which exist among and between the industrial relations systems of the countries of Western Europe, it is well to be aware of some of the characteristics which serve to differentiate the American and Canadian systems. Because these two countries have so much in common — including many of the same multinational corporations and international unions, almost all of which are headquartered in the United States — it is not surprising that their industrial relations system should be so similar, especially in the sense of placing major reliance on collective bargaining.

Among the distinguishing features that should be brought out are the differing nature of the federal or national powers in the two countries and the U.S. congressional, as distinct from the Canadian parliamentary, form of government. As for the powers of the central governments in the two countries there is really no comparison between them, particularly when it comes to control over collective bargaining and industrial relations. The Supreme Court in the U.S. has so interpreted the U.S. Constitution as to completely distort the intentions of its Founding Fathers by transferring more and more power to the federal government. Just the reverse has happened in Canada, with the result that between 90 and 95 per cent of the Canadian work force comes under provincial jurisdiction for labour relations purposes. As a result, coordination of legislation and policy is extremely difficult to achieve except during some sort of national emergency. An example is the recent period of runaway inflation when it was held that the federal government could temporarily introduce a national system of wage and price controls.

When it comes to the political activities of the labour movement the difference between the U.S. congressional form of government and Canada's parliamentary system reflects itself most visibly in the industrial relations arena. Although the American labour movement has long been closely associated with the Democratic Party, it still follows Samuel Gompers' adage of rewarding its friends and punishing its enemies. Far from being in any way apolitical, this approach makes a great deal of political sense, given the lack of party discipline within the American congressional system. The fact that the same approach makes little or no sense under a parliamentary form of government is reflected in the Canadian labour movement's closer association with the New Democratic Party. Although seldom a telling political force at the national level, this labour or social-democratic type party has held office in three provinces. In most of its activities it has served to provide organized labour with an effective spokesman in the political sphere.

Perhaps largely because of its closer relationship with a particular political party, the Canadian labour movement tends to be somewhat more ideological and reform minded that its American counterpart. This difference shows up in the positions which the CLC takes on domestic and foreign affairs. Its differences with the AFL-CIO are especially marked in the latter area. Whereas the AFL-CIO has pulled out of the International Confederation of Free Trade Unions (ICFTU), is behind the drive to have the U.S. withdraw from the ILO, and rejects virtually all contacts with the communist world, the CLC remains active in both the ICFTU and ILO and does not object to ICFTU affiliates exchanging views and visits with communist-dominated unions all over the world.

There are other distinctions between the United States and Canadian industrial relations systems, but most of these differences are of relatively minor significance. Among these differences are the greater reliance which Canada places both on law to enforce the peace obligation during the currency of a labour contract and on mandatory conciliation and mediation procedures to resolve contract renewal disputes.

VARIATIONS WITHIN WESTERN EUROPE

Industrial relations in Western Europe are much more varied than a good deal of the discussion thus far in this volume might lead one to believe. Aside from Britain, which represents an industrial relations system almost unique unto itself, there are two major types of industrial relations models in Western Europe. One is the consensual or integrationist model as best epitomized by West Germany. The other is the class conflict model as exemplified currently by France and Italy.

Before turning to these two somewhat extreme alternatives, a word or two is in order about the British system. The problem with trying to describe the British situation is that one tends to focus too much on the chaos which is so characteristic of industrial relations in the engineering industry. Many other parts of the British industrial relations system are quite settled and stable in comparison with the more troublesome sectors of the engineering industry. Although some of the blame for the poor labour relations which characterizes these sectors doubtless lies with reactionary and/or weak managements, the route of the problem clearly lies with the multiplicity of unions with overlapping jurisdictions which plague the industry. With up to twenty union groups in a single plant, many of which accept little or no control or discipline from their national union officers, it is surprising that there are not even more disputes over demarcation or jurisdictional matters and pay anomalies, distortions and inequities than there are. Clearly there is little hope for fundamental reform in Britain's most vexing industrial relations situations until a direct or indirect means is found of dealing with the problem of union fragmentation.

On the continent, Italy and, to a lesser extent, France are the two mainstays of the class-conflict or polarization models of industrial relations. In both countries major segments of the labour movement have been radicalized to the point of being willing to settle for nothing less than the total transformation of society. The unions involved are often more of a cause than an institution. They are almost invariably badly financed and on paper at least have relatively few members. They are usually ineffectual in bargaining, in large measure because this is not a priority for them. Revolution, or at least transformation, remains the ultimate goal and thus any form of accommodation with the existing order is difficult to accept. Under these circumstances even the most progressive of employers are hard pressed to maintain an effective collective bargaining relationship. The unions involved prefer to bide their time and to use their influence to set the stage for the eventual class warfare which they envisage as the only means to a solution to the capitalist problem.

At the other end of the spectrum are the Austrian and West German unions which have made sufficient progress through collective bargaining, supplemented by labour-management cooperation and political action, to accept the reform route as the best way to proceed. Unions in these countries are extremely well financed and organized. If anything they might be criticized for becoming too bureaucratic. Part of the price they have paid for the gradual but significant gains they have achieved is that they are now in a very real sense a part of the establishment. This need not present a serious problem as long as they continue to satisfy the vast majority of their memberships and there is no severe economic crisis. In Germany at least the real risk could lie in the fact that the country can in some ways be likened to a cold and efficient economic machine dedicated to growth and prosperity above all else. What happens if and when this engine breaks down could prove even more devastating for the unions than for any other groups.

To further illustrate the extreme range of industrial relations systems that are to be found in Western Europe a few more contrasts are worth drawing. Discussion at several points later in this volume will bring out the fact that Austria is probably close to a democratic corporate state. Unions and employers are both well organized and have at their disposal not only their own private central federations, but also their statutory labour and management chambers. By law all workers in Austria must belong to the Chamber of Labour and all private employers must belong to the Chamber of Management. Both Chambers are well financed by compulsory dues and operate a wide range of effective services for their members. No legislation can be passed by the Parliament in Austria until it has been submitted to these Chambers for analysis and comment. In this and other ways Austria is run on a consensual and integrative basis in which all major interest groups are fully consulted and involved. Industrial strife is almost non-existent because labour has so much influence at all levels in the system and is so well accepted by management that it seldom needs to strike to achieve its ends. Especially when a social democratic government is in office, Austria appears to demonstrate that organized labour can assume responsibility commensurate with the power it is allowed to exercise.

The state of the strongest French unions has already been stressed. Although there is often more rhetoric than substance behind the positions they take, it would appear that nothing less than a new social order will satisfy them. Aligned against them, in many instances, are well established firms still owned and operated by the families that founded them. A more reactionary group of employers would be hard to find in most cases. Often they respect neither collective agreements nor the law when it comes to labour relations, a habit or practice they are able to get away with because the unions are so preoccupied with their ideologies and philosophies that they neglect contract administration and everything else at the work place level. On the surface it would appear that no better stage could be set for revolutionary change. Yet such a revolution may well be avoided by what could emerge as a peculiar alliance between some strange bed-fellows. On the one hand, a class of professional managers is emerging in large enterprises which is dedicated to more participative styles of management and which is more than willing to experiment with various forms of industrial democracy. On the other hand, is the centre left which, with communist support, could form the next government in the country. If it nationalized all the enterprises it proposes to, it is going to have a series of colossal management problems on its hands. Such a government may have no choice but to persuade its left wing union allies to forego some of their misgivings about such concepts as codetermination and to cooperate with some of the aforementioned professional managers in trying to make an economic and financial success of its newly nationalized enterprises.

Variations on the same machinations that could shortly be taking place in France are already surfacing in Italy. Similarly, in many other countries in Western Europe a great deal of rethinking is taking place about the respective roles of labour and management. Even in Sweden, often thought to have had the most stable industrial relations climate of all, a new labour-management alignment is gradually emerging. The problem is that it is not yet clear how all these various trends in Western Europe will work themselves out. Whether there will be a general convergence of developments or whether diversity will continue to characterize the scene remains to be seen.

THE PERILS AND PITFALLS OF GENERALIZATIONS

The existing diversity in Western European industrial relations systems, as well as the questionable degree of convergence that is likely to take place in the future, makes it hazardous to generalize. This is risky even when broad comparisons are being drawn with North American developments. Yet generalize one must if one is to attempt such comparisons. In doing so one is obliged to make it clear that for every generalization there are undoubtedly many qualifications which should be added.

Britain provides an excellent case in point. One would have to live with British industrial relations for some time before one could hope to begin to fully understand them. Without appreciating the backgrounds and histories of the sundry institutions and personalities involved it is difficult to discern exactly what is going on, let alone the reasons why. This doubtless applies as well to all of the other countries involved in this survey.

All one can attempt to do is make one's generalizations as valid as possible. Even then, as the material covered thus far will no doubt have revealed, some of these generalizations will probably turn out to be somewhat misleading. Hopefully any such interpretations have been kept to a minimum throughout this volume.

Chapter 4

COLLECTIVE BARGAINING IN WESTERN EUROPE

Although preceded historically in virtually all countries in Western Europe by politically-inspired protective labour standards legislation, collective bargaining has tended to become the foremost means by which employee interests vis-a-vis their employers are promoted and protected. Increasingly, however, collective bargaining is being both supplanted to some extent and supplemented to a much greater extent by a host of other measures, including political action as well as the various other forms of industrial democracy discussed in subsequent chapters. At the same time collective bargaining itself is in the throes of a number of trends which are giving rise to many strains and stresses. Although this has not prevented its resurgence in one form or another in a number of countries, its future role throughout Western Europe remains very much a matter for conjecture.

COMPETING FORCES AND CONFLICTING TRENDS IN WESTERN EUROPEAN COLLECTIVE BARGAINING

Earlier it was noted that collective bargaining in most European countries has long been characterized by a dual level or system of negotiations. Combined with national or regional industry-by-industry bargaining there have been a host of arrangements worked out at company, plant or work levels to give life and meaning to the more central or global agreements. Complex as the totality of this overall system has been in the past, it no longer fully portrays what is going on in many countries at the present time, let alone what may happen in the future.

Some amendments or additions have to be made to this dual level model even by traditional standards of behaviour in some countries. For example, in the Scandinavian countries the central federations of labour and management have long engaged in what is known as framework bargaining. Normally this has been a bipartite process under which the major employee and employer bodies in these countries have worked out a consensus on the limits within which industry level bargaining should take place. Since either failure to agree at this supra-national level or agreement on norms beyond those which the government thinks are compatible with its forecasts for the economy can have serious repercussions for the country at large, the state sometime turns these negotiations into triangular deliberations by itself becoming a third party to them. The process, thereby, often results in triple rather than dual level negotiations. The national framework bargain is followed by a number of industry-wide negotiations, which in turn set the stage for a series of enterprise level deliberations.

Mention must also be made of certain fairly well-established forms of national or inter-industry bargaining practices in Belgium and France. Under the name of "social programming" Belgium has, since 1960, concluded a series of general or multi-industry agreements aimed at improving some of the basic living and working standards of all employees. One such agreement was designed to eliminate many of the disparities in the treatment of blue and white collar workers. Such agreements are worked out between the Federation of Belgium Enterprises and the three most representative trade union centres. Similar types of agreements have also been realized under the auspices of the National Labour Council which is made up of an equal number of management and union representatives. The costs of the advances secured under such agreements are supposed to be allowed for in negotiations at the industry level.

Ever since its traumatic experience of 1968 France too has been experimenting with national multi-industrial bargaining. Such negotiations again take place between the most representative groups of labour and management aggregations. Thus far they have embraced matters ranging from training, retraining and upgrading of manpower to income security provisions for unemployed workers beyond the age of 60.

What is even more striking about the overall collective bargaining situation in Western Europe is the extreme nature of the contrary pressures which are being brought to bear on the system. This goes back to the macro-micro tradeoff outlined in the previous chapter. On the one hand, organized labour's growing power is providing it with a more influential voice in national affairs. This is tending to involve Western European unions at the national level in what, to all intents and purposes, amounts to a form of collective bargaining with governments and, to a lesser extent, with other major interest groups in society.

On the other hand, worker dissatisfaction with the effectiveness of their union responses to their lot in life in the office or plant is compelling Western European trade unions to pay an unaccustomed degree of attention to developments at the work level. This is the main reason why many of these unions have been striving to dominate existing representative institutions at the office or plant level and/or to establish a more direct union presence among rank and file workers.

These competing forces and conflicting trends are placing labour in something of a dilemma. Organized labour has to be prepared to bargain and make commitments which may seem to short change its members in return for more say in national events. But to retain the loyalty and support of these members it must also be more responsive to their more parochial concerns. The logical way out of this seeming dilemma may lie in the distinction which can be drawn between monetary and non-monetary issues. Most of the concessions organized labour may have to make to ensure itself more influence in national developments are likely to be financial and to involve moderation and restraint in its wage and salary claims. Meanwhile it may be able to satisfy many of its rank and file membership concerns by garnering them more non-monetary gains through various forms of workers' participation, including shop floor democracy and the quality of working life.

Judging by North American experience, this could prove a very risky gamble for the unions involved. One of the reasons that American and Canadian unions are known for their bread and butter or pork chop orientation is that they have always operated on the basis of the assumption that their members' primary interest is in more take-home pay. This has tended to remain their priority objective, even though fringe benefits and other non-wage and salary items have become more important in recent years. The mentality of North American union members would still seem to be such that they would have a limited tolerance for the notion of trading off any potential wage and salary gains for more influence in decision-making of any kind. Although Western European workers appear to have a somewhat more positive attitude towards such tradeoffs, there are doubtless limits to their tolerance in this area as well.

THE ITALIAN VARIATION

To further expand upon some of the competing forces and conflicting trends that are at work in Western European collective bargaining, it is instructive to cite what seems to be happening in Italy. For years Italian collective bargaining operated primarily at the confederal or national level or by industry or sector and only secondarily at the company or plant level in a few large enterprises. This all began to change in the early 1960s, spearheaded by developments in the engineering industries. Since then, under a system known as "articulation", enterprise agreements have become an increasingly significant part of the total collective bargaining process. This shift in emphasis has corresponded with the largely spontaneous rejection by workers of the old works councils, which were thought to be management dominated, and the emergence of factory or workers' delegations, which are sometimes but not always under union auspices.

Paralleling this shift towards more worker-controlled enterprise bargaining has been an enlargement in the scope of negotiations at all levels. Some of the new issues covered by collective agreements are not that surprising because they are so work related. Examples include provisions covering everything from human adjustments made necessary by industrial conversions to measures designed to improve the quality of working life. More unusual are the growing demands for financial assistance for workers to assist them with the financing of their children's education and their family's housing. Still quite exceptional are the few instances where unions have insisted that firms place more of their new investments in the country's depressed southern region which is plagued with high levels of unemployment.

Many of these new demands are an outgrowth of two developments. One is the more united determination on the part of organized labour to seek its economic and social objectives by every means possible. The other is the seeming inability of Italy's continuing succession of divided minority governments to do very much about the country's mounting economic and social problems. Labour frustrations in the political sphere have led to union-sponsored mass demonstrations and other forms of protest designed to pressure the legislature into taking more effective and expeditious action. Failing all else, the unions have decided to use collective bargaining to force some of Italy's largest firms, such as Fiat or Olivetti, to make some progress in the above areas — even if only on the limited scale that is conceivable by this route.

More recently, as in the case of Britain, Italy's overall economic performance has been so poor that serious balance-of-payment difficulties forced it to seek the help of the International Monetary Fund (IMF). In return for such assistance the IMF drove a hard bargain with the centre-left Italian government, which now depends for its survival on communist support. Part of this bargain called for wage and salary restraint which led to more formal government involvement in the collective bargaining process. Fom both above and below Italian unions are now being pulled and pushed by the same sets of competing forces and conflicting trends that are present in so many other Western European countries.

THE SWEDISH VARIATION

Like the other Scandinavian countries the Swedish collective bargaining system has long been based on unions which are better organized at the plant level than their Western European counterparts. Although this more North American organizational structure has not spared Swedish trade unions some of the turmoil of rank and file membership restiveness experienced all over Western Europe, they seem to have been able to respond comparatively well to the challenge. Perhaps the explanation for this relatively successful response lies in the fact that Sweden is an exception to current developments in Western Europe, at least in the sense of deliberately putting even more emphasis on collective bargaining than in the past.

The continuing and increasing reliance which Swedish trade unionists seem willing to place on collective bargaining is to be attributed in large measure to the greatly increased rights they have recently secured vis-à-vis those of employers. As will be seen in a subsequent chapter, organized labour in Sweden has recently achieved minority worker representation on company boards. It has been satisfied to date with this minority status because it views its position on these boards primarily as a means to gain information and insight into company activities of concern to its work force. Together with the greatly enlarged collective bargaining rights Swedish labour has achieved for itself in recent years, access to

more information and insight is all that Swedish unions feel they so far
need to derive from company board level participation.

Organized labour's extended new bargaining rights in Sweden are
enshrined in the country's 1976 Democracy at Work Act, as it is
popularly known in English, although its proper translation is An Act for
the Joint Regulation of Working Life. How radical this legislation proves
to be remains to be seen, as its impact is gradually reconciled with
existing company law which remains intact and could conflict with it at
several points. Prevailing laws aside, there are essentially five key parts
to the new legislation. The first provides unions with much more
information about firms either as a matter of right or by request.
Employers can hold back virtually no data requested by a union, unless
they prove to the satisfaction of a court that it would be too detrimental to
the enterprises' competitive interests to release it. A second part of the
new legislation imposes on employers a primary duty to negotiate on
major changes and a secondary obligation to bargain on anything which
affects their employees. Under this provision employers do not have to
concede anything, but their plans for any changes can be delayed while
they are trying to reach an accommodation with the unions. A third
provision calls for codetermination, industrial democracy or joint
regulation agreements on virtually every aspect of employer-employee
relations not already governed by a collective agreement. Unless they
voluntarily surrender the right, unions may strike during the normal peace
obligation in order to secure such agreements, provided the issues
involved have been raised during the previous negotiations. Another part
of the legislation effectively reverses management's traditional residual
rights, except where a union or unions agree to the contrary. Otherwise
unions are granted priority of interpretation with respect to collective
agreements; codetermination, industrial democracy or joint regulation
agreements; and work assignments. Their interpretations stand until they
agree otherwise or a labour court reverses them on appeal by the
employer. Finally, the new bill grants unions veto power over the
subcontracting of work and related activities which have the effect of
transferring jobs to low wage non-union labour, thereby undermining
outstanding agreements, laws or practices.

The historical significance of these changes is that they make a decided
turning point in the long-standing understanding between Swedish unions
and employers which was eventually embodied in their famous Basic
Agreement of 1938. In return for the employers' full and open recognition

of the right of organized labour to exist and take effective action, the unions agreed to grant employers wide discretion in the area of management rights. Accordingly, Paragraph 32 of the Constitution of the Swedish Employers Confederation (SAF) barred its members from signing collective agreements which in any way restricted management's general rights to assign and organize work and to hire and fire workers. Although modified by several later agreements with the unions, Paragraph 32 remained a virtual bible of employer prerogatives until the recent legislation was enacted.

The new law obviously holds out great promise for union advances. This is why the labour movement has terminated all its old agreements with the employer's federation and is now seeking a series of new more advantageous ones. Although management interests do not deny the enormous potential inherent in the new legislation from labour's point of view, they stress that it has yet to be realized. For the most part the new bill is facilitative and permissive and, in and of itself, does not force employers to concede very much. Accordingly the next few months and years will be a critical testing period under the new legislation. Having just concluded a difficult round of wage and salary bargaining, Swedish unions and employers are now engaged in a series of negotiations under the new law designed to replace their old voluntary agreements, as well as to accommodate a number of new labour demands ranging across the entire industrial democracy spectrum.

Given the economic and political uncertainty now plaguing Sweden, it is difficult to predict what will result from these negotiations. The opening positions of the parties are quite far apart in most areas, but they seem to want to work out their differences if only to avoid more detailed statutory regulation. Employers fear more legislative inroads on their prerogatives and rights, and unions are concerned lest a trend toward more legal intervention should reduce their autonomy and independence. These mutual fears and concerns may well lead labour and management to compromise their differences sufficiently to make the new law's heightened reliance on collective bargaining pay off.

FUTURE DEVELOPMENTS

By now it should be clear that, in one form or another and at one level or another, collective bargaining is still thriving in most parts of Western

Europe. Defined in its broadest sense, collective bargaining in Western Europe will doubtless expand in scope. No matter what the form or level at which it is practiced collective bargaining will thus be called upon to deal with more and more issues.

At the same time collective bargaining will normally only be envisaged as a necessary and not as a sufficient means of promoting worker interests. Political action will remain important as will the other forms of industrial democracy discussed later. How collective bargaining can be internally reconciled in its different forms and at its various levels, let alone with other forms of worker representation, remains to be seen. The outcome in each country will undoubtedly depend on overall socio-economic-political developments which go far beyond the scope of this volume.

One can only speculate about the future even where the trend of events seems quite clear-cut. For example, recent Swedish experience would seem to suggest that an expansion of information rights and an enlargement of the scope of collective bargaining, together with a narrowing and shrinking of management prerogatives, can provide a potent means of extending the influence of organized workers in enterprise decision-making. Time alone will allow one to determine whether this indeed proves to be the case.

The haunting problem which remains concerns the ways in which organized labour will deploy and use its new-found powers, whether in the traditional collective bargaining sphere or elsewhere. Organized labour has yet to prove that it can take on more power and exercise it responsibly at any or all levels of decision-making, while still remaining democratic and responsive to its membership. This challenge becomes all the more telling as unions become more engrossed in management decision-making and the managerial process in general. One has to query how far union leaders can pursue this course without themselves becoming managers with all the consequences this could entail.

Chapter 5

ORGANIZED LABOUR AND NATIONAL ECONOMIC AND SOCIAL POLICY FORMULATION

In the long run there is probably no more critical level of industrial democracy from organized labour's point of view than at the national level. This is because anything accomplished or not accomplished on labour's behalf at other levels of industrial democracy can be offset by overall national developments. This is why the labour movement, like every other effective interest group in society, must take an active interest in the development of general economic and social policy.

LIMITATIONS ON ORGANIZED LABOUR'S PARTICIPATION IN NATIONAL ECONOMIC AND SOCIAL POLICY FORMULATION

It is essential to stress at the beginning the necessary limitations on any group other than government when it comes to the formulation of national economic and social policy. In any state based on democratic and responsible government the ultimate arbitrator or interpreter of the public interest must be the elected government acting through the national legislatures in accordance with the country's constitution. To suggest otherwise is to negate the ultimate sovereignty of the majority of a people's elected representatives, assuming again that they are acting within their constitutional limitations.

Subject to its sovereign powers and ultimate responsibility for the public interest any government should be free to consult all manner of interested groups about the way in which it is conducting and is planning to conduct a country's affairs. By the same token it is equally appropriate for all such groups to seek such consultation on as meaningful and significant a basis as possible. For them to do otherwise is to do less than they conceivably could for those they represent.

Traditionally most interest groups have relied on a mixture of formal and informal means to try to influence the direction of public policies of concern to their members. As the next section will reveal, there are a variety of formal mechanisms which organized labour and other groups may utilize to this end. Sometimes these mechanisms are essentially bipartite or dual in nature, in the sense of involving interaction between only one interest group at a time and the government. Increasingly they tend to involve labour, management and government as well as, in some instances, other influential elements in society and thus become tripartite or multipartite in character. More difficult to delineate and explore are the numerous informal consultative channels which exist between labour and government and other groups in society.

The dangerous and delicate dividing line in all of these processes occurs when consultation begins to give way to codecision-making. It is at this point that the risk of the corporate state — democratic or otherwise — becomes a very real possibility. Certainly consultation by governments with various interest groups should be a decisive factor in some cases and be influential at all times. But such consultation should never become such a binding force on a government that it loses its freedom of action as the elected majority choice of the people. It is at this point that democracy can all too easily give way to a corporate state in which the interplay of power blocs begins to replace the electoral process as the predominant variable in all decision-making. Such a state may simply represent a more indirect form of democracy via greater citizen participation in the various power blocs whose interaction tends to supplant the legislative process. But such a state may also lead to such a concentration of power in the hands of a few leading power brokers that it degenerates into a form quite inconsistent with anything resembling a democracy.

ALTERNATIVE FORMS OF UNION INFLUENCE IN NATIONAL ECONOMIC AND SOCIAL POLICY FORMULATION

There are many ways in which the labour movement can influence the formulation of national economic and social policy. Collective bargaining itself can have either a direct or an indirect bearing on such policy formulation. Indirectly and superficially the so-called free collective bargaining system may seem to run its own independent course. But as in the case of price setting and other income determining processes, wage and salary negotiations may bring to bear cost-push pressures which force a government to introduce offsetting deflationary measures.

If cost-push pressures emanating from collective bargaining and other elements in the total economic system become serious enough, governments may feel compelled to introduce various forms of income policies including wage controls. Any such controls naturally tend to abort the normal collective bargaining process between unions and employers and to force the former to concentrate their attention on the government. To the extent that wage controls leave any room for negotiations by unions it is with the state rather than with private or even quasi-public enterprises.

Increasing resort by governments to income policies of various kinds has added immensely to the historical rationale for unions to become deeply involved in political action. As earlier explained in the case of the United States, even labour movements which have appeared — if not professed — to be almost apolitical are anything but that when one examines their actual record. This is hardly surprising since so much of what governments are engaged in can have either an adverse or a beneficial effect on labour. This basic fact of political life is becoming the more obvious as governments involve themselves in more and more facets of society.

Given the ideological and philosophic orientation of so many unions in Western Europe, they have long been committed to the support of particular political parties. Even when some of these unions claim to be neutral they usually champion the political party which comes closest to favouring their point of view. Most of the labour movement in Western Europe is openly committed to either social democratic or communist parties. In France and Italy the bulk of the labour movement appears to believe that their long-run objectives can best be met by political action rather than collective bargaining. To this segment of Western European organized labour the only effective long-run way to influence national economic and social policy formulation is perceived to be through political action. To most of this faction this means striving for eventual electoral victory through democracy via the ballot box. To others, less patient in nature and more revolutionary in spirit, it implies class and industrial warfare and anything else which will speed up the overthrow of the existing order.

Where organized labour's political allies have achieved office there is no doubt that its influence has been very much enhanced. This has proven especially true in Scandinavia where, in Sweden, for example, the labour movement was undoubtedly by far the most influential interest group during the recently terminated four decades of government by that country's social democratic party. Aside from the risk that its political allies may not be able to achieve or maintain themselves in office, there is another reason why unions may wish to strengthen other mechanisms for inter-group consultation with whatever party is in power. When labour's political allies are in office it can turn out to be a very sobering experience. British labour has been in the process of discovering just how sober this experience can prove. Despite a Labour government it has been asked to make and is making sacrifices that it would probably never countenance under any other government, even if the economic situation was just as desperate.

Within the liberal democratic market economy framework there are many consultative arrangements which can be introduced at the national level to facilitate labour participation in public policy formulation. Despite the range of possibilities that exists in this area and the ongoing thrust of developments at lower levels of industrial democracy, comparatively little progress has been made in this field at the national level in many countries of Western Europe. In part this may be due to a reluctance by governments and political parties to share any more of their power than they are compelled to. In part it also doubtless reflects the fact that some unions will not collaborate in any way with governments to which they are opposed. It may also simply be that labour has thus far been concentrating most of its efforts in the field of industrial democracy at the industry, corporation and plant level. In any event, organized labour in most Western European countries has only recently become involved in formal consultative procedures for influencing overall government policies.

The situation is much more complex when it comes to informal arrangements intended to influence government thinking. For the most part none of these channels are mentioned in the remarks below concerning individual countries because they are often so arranged as to defy ready identification, let alone careful scrutiny. They range from discreet meetings and telephone calls, through reliance on all sorts of trusted intermediaries, to quite open and above board breakfasts, luncheons and dinners in favoured restaurants. These contacts are obviously important in any on-going system of decision-making. They should not be neglected even where more formal arrangements exist, supposedly to serve the same purpose. There comes a point in virtually every decision-making process where nothing less than face-to-face contact among a few key leaders will suffice to break a deadlock and make some progress. The results seldom emerge where they are achieved, but that hardly matters. The point is that there is no substitute at times for informal gatherings, even though they may seem almost clandestine in view of the secrecy which must often surround them. Gatherings such as these produce the makings of the face-saving formulas, which all involved then find it possible to accept in more public fora.

BRITAIN'S SOCIAL CONTRACT

Britain's famous social contract illustrates how much influence and power a labour movement can wield over a friendly government, at least temporarily if not on a more permanent basis. It is essential in trying to understand the recent British situation to appreciate the derivation of its social contract and why it has held together in one form or another for as long as it has. The social contract had its beginnings prior to the Labour Party's return to office in 1974. During the term of office of the previous Conservative government the labour movement, under the auspices of the Trade Union Congress (TUC) and the Labour Party, established a liaison committee to try to improve the basis for their relationship. The latter had deteriorated badly during the prior Labour Party Administration due to a serious split over industrial relations policy which helped to ensure the subsequent defeat of the government.

As the social contract evolved over the years it became a commitment on the part of the labour movement to restrain its pay claims under a Labour government in return for a host of concessions favourable to both low-paid workers and other low-income recipients and the unions themselves. The basis for this agreement became all the more telling when the Labour Party was re-elected in 1974 in the throes of a period of rampant and runaway inflation. Without going into the details it can be said that within a year or so the labour movement did begin to live up to its side of the bargain by persuading many of its members to accept real wage cuts, which in the case of the skilled trades turned out to be quite drastic. The Labour government responded for its part with food subsidies, price and rent controls, tax concessions for those with low incomes, and a host of pro-labour laws the like of which Britain had never seen before.

The government's first act on the legislative front was to rescind the union-hated Industrial Relations Act which the Conservative government had introduced in 1971 in an attempt to reform British industrial relations by imposing a North American type legal framework. Thereafter there followed a spate of bills including the Employment Protection Act, the Health & Safety at Work Act, the Social Securities Pension Act and the Sex Discrimination Act—to mention the most noteworthy of them. This legislation reversed Britain's traditional reliance on the doctrine of state abstention in the field of industrial relations. It created a number of new labour standards and granted unions many of the privileges and rights which they had favoured under the Conservative Party's Industrial Relations Act, while removing virtually all of the responsibilities and restrictions they had bitterly resisted. The government also established the Bullock Commission whose report on how best to grant the TUC's demands for codetermination — which formed another part of the social contract — is discussed in some detail in Chapter 7.

By now it should be obvious that Britain's social contract is anything but a simple document. It is a complicated series of undertakings by labour's union and political wings that defies brief analysis or description. Nonetheless there are a few salient points that should be made about this experiment in public policy formulation. The first, of course, is that it is an experiment and no more than that as yet. Although it has already endured for longer than many observers and participants anticipated, it has no assured future, mainly because one side of the bargain, the Labour Party, cannot count on retaining office that much longer.

A second point to be made is that the social contract was born in a crisis and has been successively renewed each year during a series of interrelated crises. The original crisis was more political than economic, while the subsequent crises have been just the reverse. Initially the social contract grew out of a family feud between the two branches of labour — that is, its trade union and political wings — which had to be healed in order for the Labour Party to demonstrate sufficient public credibility to regain office. Ever since returning to power the government has been plagued by stagflation and balance of payments problems. This continuing economic crisis forced it to resort to a large IMF loan in return for which it had to pledge continuing anti-inflationary measures, partly through the device of its social contract with the unions.

A third point to be made is that the social contract is proving harder and harder to defend on the union side. Understandably, increasing numbers of the skilled trades are in open revolt against their union leaders because of the slippage in their differentials as well as the sharp fall in their real incomes. The mass of workers is growing more skeptical about the whole business because their restraint has not paid off in terms of any improvement in the economy. So far neither pay restraint nor cutbacks in government spending seem to have been translated into additional investment and employment, as they were apparently supposed to be.

It is going to be increasingly difficult, because of these considerations, to keep coming up with new rounds of the social contract. So many anomalies, distortions and inequities on the wage and salary side have been built up by the combinations of ceilings, across-the-board adjustments, and tax concessions which have been introduced that it would cost a small fortune to correct them. It is also increasingly questionable how many more non-monetary concessions the government can grant to the unions in return for them trying to persuade their members to put up with still more rounds of pay restraint.

A final point to be made about the British social contract is that it is essentially bipartite in nature. Although the Confederation of British Industry (CBI) has been well aware of developments throughout the period of the social contract, it has never been a party to it. For the most part management's participation in the social contract has been quite indirect. Essentially it has only been involved via the government's price controls which are used to compel employers to ensure that no unions or workers are granted more than the wage and salary increases due them under the contract.

The only formal tripartite mechanism for policy consultation at the national level in Britain exists in the form of the National Economic Development Commission or "Neddy" as it is popularly known. This body emerged in the early 1960s and, under the chairmanship of the Chancellor of the Exchequer or the Prime Minister, has had a history of ups and downs. With its staff of 250 economists and other experts, Neddy generates a great deal of data, a lot of ideas, and many position papers. Together with the numerous little Neddies which exist for most industries, this whole institutional apparatus is now intended to be at the centre of the notion of a national industrial strategy for the country. This strategy is to be based on a series of tripartite company and industry planning agreements, but very few of these have emerged to date.

All too often so far Neddy has served as little more than a forum within which the major interest groups articulate their usual positions. Its meetings are usually too large and unwieldy and its agendas too detailed and specific. Despite all these handicaps, the institution has proved useful on occasion, if only as one of the few channels of communication left open during highly strained periods of industrial conflict.

If Britain is to develop a sustainable format through which labour can have a continuing and effective input into national policy formulation, it is more likely to occur through a reformed and revitalized multipartite Neddy than a bipartite social contract. The latter is so closed an arrangement that it is actually very risky for labour. After all, if the country continues downhill under the social contract the public has no one to blame but labour, whether in its political or trade union guise. One of the lessons to be drawn from recent British experience would appear to be that organized labour cannot expect any more permanent influence on national policy formulation than it is prepared to concede to other major interest groups.

THE NETHERLANDS SITUATION

Ever since World War II industrial democracy at the national level in the Netherlands has revolved around the Foundation of Labour and the Social and Economic Council. The Foundation had its beginnings during the concentration camp days of wartime occupation and is a bipartite voluntary body which was jointly established by labour and management. It was characterized, in its early years, by a high degree of cooperation between the parties as they worked with the government to rebuild the country's war-torn economy. As part of this effort the unions agreed in the Foundation to many years of modest national rounds of pay increases. This era came to an abrupt end with the dramatic wage explosion which began in 1963 and continued for several years thereafter, as union members rebelled against their leaders and forced them to become more aggressive in their demands. Throughout the 1970s the Foundation has found it increasingly difficult to arrive at a national framework agreement. During this period the national pattern has often emerged only after a series of industry-wide strikes.

Even more intriguing has been the changing role of the government. For years after the war it could count on the self-restraint of the parties and labour, in particular, to ensure modest pay settlements consistent with its macro interpretation of economic developments in the country. It did establish the now-defunct Board of Government Mediators to administer the framework agreements reached in the Foundation, but that was about all it had to do. More recently the government has found itself embroiled in everything from a modest type of social contract to wage and price controls. The closest facsimile to Britain's social contract seems to have emerged from the last two rounds of national wage and salary negotiations. Informally and unofficially the government agreed on both occasions to reduce the burden of social security premiums on employers in order to induce them to raise their pay offers sufficiently to satisfy the unions. On at least two other occasions — one during the height of the oil crisis — the government has imposed a settlement on the parties.

Despite this recent record of discord and government intervention, the Foundation of Labour appears to remain a body of some importance. Although less consensual and more conflictual in nature, it still provides the major forum for attempting to resolve labour-management differences. Currently, for example, it is working on a number of joint studies growing out of the last trying round of negotiations. The central issue in that round was the employers' demand for the termination of the full indexing of wages and salaries in relation to the rising cost of living. The employers felt that this escalator clause was undermining the country's competitive position by aggravating the inflationary spiral. The unions agreed to a thorough investigation of the issues involved in return for one more year of indexing. The Foundation is also studying the relationship between wage and salary restraint and profit, investment and employment in order to try to agree on a formula which will ensure that, if agreed to, moderation in pay claims does in fact lead to more employment. Still another study is being undertaken on a variety of questions pertaining to the quality of working life.

The Social and Economic Council is a statutory tripartite body composed of three equal parts. Labour and management each have one third of the members, while the other third is made up of "crown members" who are independent experts in various fields. Although this Council has some administrative responsibilities in relation to the mandatory works councils in the country and some other agencies, it is basically an advisory and consultative body. So influential has it become in this latter capacity over the years, that it would be unthinkable for the government to bring in any new economic or social legislation before referring it to the Council for analysis and comment. The Council also prepares an annual report on the state of the country's economic and social affairs, which it tends to use as the basis for its reaction to the government's macro plan for the year ahead.

Reflecting the impasses that have precluded framework agreements in the Foundation of Labour, the Social and Economic Council has run into more difficulty during the past few years in trying to realize a consensus on several issues. Even so it has managed to find compromises on issues as contentious as codetermination on company supervisory boards and health and safety regulations. Although some concern has been expressed about the future of the Council, a current study of its operation is unlikely to produce any major suggestions for change. It is almost certain to remain an important part of the Netherlands' system for national economic and social policy formulation, whether or not it is subject to any modifications.

It is well to conclude this section by stressing that under the Netherlands system the government and parliament have the last word. Although this has always been the case formally and legally, it has been reinforced in practice of late by the magnitude of the conflict and divisions between unions and employers. The postwar years of consensus have given way to successive years of confrontation and the government has increasingly found itself caught between two sets of polarized protagonists. Since 1970, when it first introduced a new law on wage regulation, the government has intervened intermittently in the collective bargaining process. Currently, when the cabinet presents its national budget, it also presents its views on what it would deem appropriate wage and price and related adjustments. If labour and management cannot agree within the Foundation of Labour on a wage round consistent with this government suggested framework there then ensues a complicated round of discussions involving all three parties. Throughout this process the government hinges its final budgetary proposals on a satisfactory wage round. It is in this sense that the Netherlands could be moving in the direction of something more akin to the British social contract, but with management as well as labour participating in the interaction process with government.

AUSTRIA'S PARITY COMMISSION ON PRICES AND WAGES

The role of Austria's unique labour and management chambers was highlighted in an earlier chapter. It will be recalled that no legislation is supposed to be passed by the Austrian Parliament until these chambers have had a chance to pass judgment on it. For the most part the two chambers operate quite independently in this respect, although they often find themselves united in their positions for or against a government proposition. Where they are united one way or the other that usually decides the matter.

Perhaps even more unique to Austria is its Parity Commission for Wages and Prices which may best be described as a mixed private-public body. In some ways it appears to be strictly a bipartite labour-management body with limited consultative powers. In fact it appears to be much more than that, if only because it is chaired by the Chancellor and attended by senior government officials. Moreover, although it is a voluntary joint body it operates under a quasi-legislative sanction, since the Prices Regulation Act authorizes it to pass judgment on a wide range of prices which are normally not increased without the approval of its Subcommittee on Prices. The Parity Commission's Subcommittee on Wages discusses the desirable overall level of wage and salary increases in the country. The Parity Commission, or its Subcommittee on Wages, actually functions as a kind of master nationwide negotiating forum establishing the overall pay framework, which no unions and employers are supposed to exceed without special justification.

To assist it in these tasks and to help it prepare its views on even broader economic and social concerns, the Parity Commission has created an Advisory Committee on Economic and Social Questions composed of experts from a wide range of groups, including the government, special research institutes, and the universities, as well as labour and management. Combined with the resources of the labour and management chambers, this Advisory Council provides the Parity Commission with the capacity to offer its advice to the government on virtually any matter of mutual concern to employees and employers.

The problem with the Austrian system is to ascertain how it actually operates. In many respects, as was mentioned earlier, Austria appears to be a corporate state, albeit a democratic one. Most groups in the country are well organized and well represented where it seems to count the most. As a result consensus politics is the order of the day and of life in general in Austria. And yet this is a country where institutional arrangements do not begin to explain the entire situation. Despite the plethora of formal mechanisms for interaction that exist, most of the real action appears to take place behind the scenes among a relatively small number of the leaders of the key interest groups in the country. Related facets of this fascinating Austrian system of decision-making will be brought out in later chapters, especially in the one on "Industrial Democracy and the Future of Labour and Management".

WEST GERMANY'S CONCERTED ACTION COMMITTEE

Despite its pioneering role in other areas of industrial democracy West

Germany was slow to move at the national level. This was doubtless largely due to the country's successful dependence on the enterprise or market system for its postwar recovery. West Germany also established a tradition of non-government involvement in the industrial relations sphere where it came to rely instead on the common sense of the social partners themselves.

Ever since West Germany began to move towards the establishment of its Concerted Action Committee the emphasis has been on the achievement of something approaching a consensus rather than on the realization of specific agreements. The first step in this direction took place in 1963 when the government established an independent Council of Economic Advisers to provide the basis for an intelligent public discussion of the general state of the economy. Whenever this Council reports, the government is obliged to submit its reports as well as its own responses to them to Parliament and thus to the public at large.

The Concerted Action Committee brings together representatives of labour, management, the government and the central bank for periodic reviews of the economic outlook. It has had a somewhat chequered history. Shortly after it was established in the mid 1960s, labour and management both were of the opinion that it had been created primarily as a device to try to gain their joint approval for pre-determined government policies. Since then there have been occasions when labour in particular has felt that the Committee was being used to promote a specific wage target for the economy as a whole, something which is an anathema to some of the major unions.

Although the Concerted Action Committee has varied in its significance over the past few years it still serves as a focal point for discussions by the social partners with the government and central bank about the general trend of economic events. The object is not a precise figure for wages or prices or anything else, but rather some undertaking about the more or less desirable limits within which these major economic variables should move. Sometimes the results are remarkably close to those discussed in the Committee, but this is hardly enough in itself to prove or disprove its worth.

As in the case of many of the other national bipartite consultative bodies discussed in this chapter, probably the most important attribute of West Germany's Concerted Action Committee is its availability in times of economic crisis as a forum for the parties to try to find some common ground on what should be done. The Committee emerged during just such a crisis and seems to function most meaningfully in this kind of atmosphere.

BELGIUM IN A STATE OF FLUX

The present situation in Belgium is best described as confusing when it comes to the labour movement's involvement in national public policy formulation. The long-standing bipartite National Council of Labour is invariably consulted on all proposed industrial relations legislation. Moreover labour and management often take the initiative in this field and in the extension of employment standards. They may take such initiatives either through the National Council of Labour or through the many parity commissions which operate on an industry basis with equal and joint representation from both sides, together with a neutral chairman and vice chairman appointed by the government. Nationally this system has produced about thirty statutes, pertaining to everything from minimum wages to sickness pay, which were agreed on by the parties and subsequently ratified by the government and parliament.

In the wider economic and social sphere there now appear to be two or three competing and overlapping national consultative bodies. One is the long-established Central Economic Council which, in keeping with its wider jurisdiction than the National Labour Council, includes independent experts and consumer spokesmen as well as labour and management representatives. Another is the tripartite National Committee on Economic Expansion which is chaired by the Minister of Economic Affairs and which is intended to provide advice on major economic and social issues. This Committee seems to have fallen into abeyance and to have been replaced in part by the Steering Committee of the National Conference on Employment, which came into being on a more or less ad hoc basis as unemployment became a more serious problem.

The main reason for the state of flux in these areas in Belgium appears to be that the government has tended, until recently at least, to be more concerned about inflation than unemployment, while the labour movement is of the reverse persuasion. For the moment Belgian management is caught in the middle of this struggle over priorities, but tends to be aligned with the government, if only because of its fears about the country's competitive position. Regardless of how these priorities are worked out, some form of bipartite and tripartite consultation will doubtless survive at the national level in Belgium because it is now such a well-established tradition in the country.

FORM AND SUBSTANCE IN FRANCE

France has, on paper, what would appear to be one of the more grandiose systems for wide national interest-group participation in economic and social policy development. At the centre of this system is the Economic and Social Council made up of an extremely wide range of power blocs. The government is supposed to consult the Council on all its major economic and social plans. In addition, the Council has the right to present its views on all manner of subjects to the appropriate parliamentary committees. The Council also has a variety of links with other government and quasi-government bodies involved in forecasting and planning.

The problem is that the Council does not appear to be either very active or respected. The government seldom seems to take it very seriously and, presumably in large measure because of this, many of the groups represented on the Council do not invest a great deal of time and effort in its work. About all one can say about the French system is that it has a great deal of potential. Whether that potential will ever be realized is anyone's guess.

THE SWEDISH VARIATION

At least until recently Sweden has been looked upon as a model of social partnership and tripartitism. It gained this reputation despite the absence of anything like a national economic and social consultative body. From organized labour's point of view there really was no need for any such body while its political ally, the Social Democratic Party, remained in power over the last four decades. In addition, until recently the union's close links with the government were in a way complemented by the Basic Agreement they had with the employers governing their interrelationships.

Even with the Social Democratic Party out of office and the Basic Agreement with the employers rescinded, the labour movement in Sweden does not appear to feel the need for any formalized central bipartite or tripartite consultative agency. This is doubtless because Sweden has a variety of other means to serve the same end. In the first place the Swedish legislative process entails a high degree of consultation among and between all the major interest groups likely to be affected by any significant new statutory measures. Well before any such laws are introduced, let alone enacted, special committees are set up to consider the issues involved. These committees include spokesmen for the major interest groups as well as representatives of the political parties. Their task is to explore the pros and cons of the proposed new legislative enactments and to see if they can arrive at an agreement or consensus about what should be done. Where they cannot find a satisfactory compromise — as in the case of the committee that was established to examine the issues raised by Sweden's new Democracy at Work Law — these committees issue majority and minority reports. That the government and parliament are in no way bound by the results of this consultative process was demonstrated in the case of the Democracy at Work Act which hewed much closer to the minority labour report than to the majority report on the subject.

As will be indicated in the next chapter, specifically in the case of its National Labour Market Board, Swedish labour is also involved with management in a number of important semi-autonomous public administrative agencies. Although these bodies are primarily administrative in character, they also offer advice and counsel on a wide range of issues related to their particular spheres of activity. In addition, of course, there is the usual extensive informal consultation that takes place between the government and the major power blocs on a non-institutional basis.

Whether organized labour will continue to be satisfied with these various channels of influence under a government controlled by parties other than its social democratic ally remains to be seen. There is considerable friction between the labour movement and the new government, but neither side appears likely to disturb the status quo that much. Should that happen all concerned might decide that Sweden requires more formal and institutionalized machinery for consultation on the development of national economic and social policies than it already has.

Regardless of which political party is in power, perhaps the major impetus for such machinery will come from the growing interdependence of wage and price determination and government fiscal, monetary and related policies. Although Swedish labour and management both seem eager to preserve their autonomy and independence from government encroachment of one kind or another, they are unlikely to be able to do so unless they more effectively coordinate their activities with those of government. To this end they may find it preferable to participate in some sort of a meaningful economic and social council than to lose more and more control over their affairs by default to the government.

CONCLUSION

Organized labour is bound to insist on more influence in broad national policy formulation in return for some moderation and restraint in its wage and salary demands. This is the essence of the macro-micro tradeoff alluded to in an earlier chapter.

Western European experience in this area indicates no overall formal or institutional pattern. There are countries, such as Austria, where there is seemingly continuous consultation in one form or another; while there are others, such as France, where little or no meaningful consultation takes place except in an emergency. In between are countries like Holland and Belgium where long-standing consultative arrangements are still active but in the midst of some changes. Meanwhile Britain has its social contract, which could prove quite temporary, and Sweden has its alternative approach, which worked fairly well under forty years of social democratic rule but could prove more fragile under an alternative government. Unmentioned has been Italy where, as noted in an earlier chapter, the unions seem to have chosen to bargain rather than consult with the government over the issues which divide them.

Before concluding this chapter, reference should be made to the Economic and Social Committee of the European Communities, including primarily the European Economic Community. Modeled after the French Economic and Social Council this Committee is composed of three groups of representatives — labour, management, and various other interest groups besides the governments which are not represented on this body. Without going into the details of the operations of the European Economic Community and the various other European communities, it will suffice to note that the Economic and Social Committee has to be consulted on a wide range of issues before any action is taken. Although apparently more influential within its context than its French equivalent, this Committee also leaves something to be desired (according to those close to it). All the same, if, as and when it evolves into a more influential body, it could become an intra-country model for inter-country emulation.

Finally, mention should again be made of informal channels of communication and direct political action. No amount of formal institutional consultative machinery will ever replace or supplant these avenues of influence. For organized labour in particular, representing as it does vast numbers of the electorate, there will always be the temptation to rely first and foremost on its personal contacts and potential political clout. This means that any form of national consultation in public policy formulation must be perceived by labour as being effective and meaningful before it will place any confidence or faith in it.

Chapter 6

JOINT OR TRIPARTITE ADMINISTRATION OF SELECTED PUBLIC PROGRAMS

The last chapter began with a warning about the limitations which should apply to organized labour and other interest groups in the development of national economic and social policies which must remain the ultimate responsibility of government in a democratic society. Few such limitations, other than overall scrutiny by the public authorities, need apply to the administration of such policies insofar as it may be deemed desirable by government to delegate their management to such groups. Although governments have been more than willing to involve labour and management and other groups in an advisory and consultative capacity in the administration of such programs, some governments have been fairly leery about going any further than this.

It should be added that neither labour nor management in most countries have been pressing governments for more than an advisory and consultative role in these areas. Accordingly this tends to be an even more neglected level of industrial democracy than that discussed in the previous chapter. This general tendency has not precluded some major developments in this field in a few countries which are gradually beginning to have a telling effect in others. In any event this chapter looks beyond the more traditional advisory and consultative role to some examples where joint labour-management, tripartite labour-management-government, or other multipartite administrative arrangements have been introduced for a range of public programs.

WESTERN EUROPE'S TRIPARTITE LABOUR COURTS

Labour courts in most Western European countries are the one public agency where tripartition is usually the norm. As was noted in an earlier chapter these labour courts have no real parallel in North America, although they do bring to mind the latter's familiar labour relations boards and less common tripartite arbitration boards. Unlike North American labour relations boards, Western European labour courts seldom if ever have any jurisdiction over anything like the North American union certification or recognition procedures. Nor are they involved in the wide array of unfair labour practices that characterize the North American legislative framework for the conduct of industrial relations. Almost the only major North American type of unfair labour practice over which some Western European labour courts have jurisdiction is illegal strikes occurring during the peace obligation which prevails while a collective agreement is in effect.

For the most part these labour courts deal with disputes arising from contracts of employment concerning the rights of individuals. Such disputes may arise under an applicable collective agreement or pertinent labour statute, and normally may be brought forward either by the aggrieved individual on his or her own behalf or with the support of his or her union or works council. For the most part it is the unions which bring these cases before the labour courts. The vast majority of such cases entail claims by individual workers against their employers over pay, dismissals or redundancies.

As far as broader union-management disputes over the interpretation of collective agreements a few labour courts in Western Europe have some jurisdiction, while others have none. This is a highly contentious issue in many countries because of the reluctance of unions and sometimes employers to have the results of their negotiations applied and enforced by any third party. Many unions also object to the general idea of the peace obligation which is laid down by law in several countries to apply during the life of a collective agreement.

Given the importance of labour courts in many Western European countries to unions and employers as well as individual employees, it is hardly surprising that labour and management should play a major part in their administration. Usually these courts are tripartite in composition with a government-named lawyer as chairperson and an equal number of labour and management lay or side members. Decisions are naturally by majority rule, but are often unanimous. Where appeals are permitted to higher level labour courts or the normal civil courts there is a tendency to move away from the tripartite format; but this is generally accepted as the issues at these higher levels frequently only revolve around narrow points of law and legal interpretation.

MANPOWER AND SOCIAL SECURITY ADMINISTRATION IN WEST GERMANY

One of the critical elements in the West German concept of a social partnership between labour and management lies in their joint control and finance of the major manpower and social security programs in the country. Included in this range of jointly sponsored social services are everything from health insurance and old age pensions to unemployment insurance and the full range of manpower programs. All of these services are administered by self-governing public corporations which enjoy a high degree of organizational and financial autonomy.

An illustration of such a corporation which is worthy of examination is the Federal Employment Institute. This corporation has a governing body composed of thirteen representatives from each of the two social partners, in addition to another thirteen independent or neutral officials drawn from within the Institute itself and other public bodies. Beneath the governing body is an executive board of nine members constituted along the same lines. Similar committees, but of a more advisory and consultative nature, are associated with the Institute's nine regional and 146 local offices. Labour and management interest in the success of the Institute's operations is heightened by the fact that they share the costs of the services it provides via payroll deductions. Only when unemployment rises above a specified level does the government contribute any public funds and then only to cover the extra insurance payments required.

West Germany's Federal Employment Institute provides just about as comprehensive a range of manpower services as are to be found anywhere in the world. Aside from managing the country's placement and unemployment insurance system, it administers its adult training, retraining and upgrading programs, and is responsible for vocational guidance in the public schools. Because of their joint concern about the cost and effectiveness of these activities both labour and management strive to ensure that the Institute maintains an efficient high-quality service.

To appreciate the magnitude of the task that labour and management have assumed in their joint administration of West Germany's overall manpower and social security systems it need only be noted that the funds involved add up to over ¼ of the country's gross national product. Since the vast majority of these funds are raised by social security premiums levied on employees and employers, they have a mutual interest in ensuring that they are well spent. They do this in the context of an underlying belief in and dedication to the proposition that the country's long-run well-being depends on a healthy, secure and skilled population and work force.

SWEDEN'S NATIONAL LABOUR MARKET BOARD

Sweden's National Labour Market Board clearly represents that country's major contribution to the concept of jointly administered public programs. This Board is responsible for the full range of Sweden's widely heralded active labour market policy, which in some ways is even more comprehensive than that of West Germany's. As in the latter's case the Swedish Board administers the country's public employment service with all of its ancillary activities including unemployment insurance, vocational guidance and so on. A special feature of the Swedish system which has yet to demonstrate its full potential is its investment reserve program. This program grants firms significant tax concessions in return for setting aside funds from current profits for later voluntary reinvestment in regions or at times the Labour Market Board deems appropriate in order to stimulate employment.

The composition of the National Labour Market Board differs from that of the governing body and executive board in the West German Employment Institute in a number of respects. First of all there is not parity of labour and management representation. Instead there are twice as many union as employer representatives, a ratio which does not seem to have concerned management interests in the country. Presumably this is because the Board is basically an administrative body which operates largely on the basis of consensus within a policy framework laid down by the statute creating it. In addition to the six labour and three management representatives on the National Board, the Director General and Deputy Director General as well as two elected staff representatives are full-fledged members. Finally there are two independent or neutral members nominated by the government. A somewhat similar composition prevails at the county labour board level, where again as in West Germany the boards are more advisory and consultative in character than the national board.

Although the work of the National Labour Market Board has been generally acclaimed in the past both within and beyond Sweden, some disillusionment has occurred during the past two or three years. This disenchantment is to be attributed largely to the rising level of unemployment in the country, a trend which in turn appears to be due in large measure to an attempt to raise general living standards faster than the performance and productivity improvement of the economy will permit. Not even the most advanced and sophisticated active labour market policies can be expected to accomplish very much when unemployment is being pushed up by basic underlying economic forces.

Despite some disappointment with its active labour market policies, organized labour has not demanded any basic changes in the composition and functions of the labour market board. It thus appears destined to remain the leading example of non-governmental management of public programs in Sweden, although this is a practice which is followed in varying degrees in many other areas of public administration in the country.

BRITAIN'S ADVISORY CONCILIATION AND ARBITRATION SERVICE

Recently Britain has established a number of multi-party bodies to administer some of its public services other than its nationalized industries. Aside from the Industrial Tribunals (the British equivalent of the continental labour courts) and the Manpower Services Commission (which is the country's closest, but still distant, counterpart to the Federal Employment Institute in West Germany and the National Labour Market Board in Sweden), the most instructive example of this trend is to be found in the form of Britain's Advisory Conciliation and Arbitration Services (ACAS).

This quasi-independent government or public body is financed under the national budget, but administered by a tripartite body made up of an equal number of labour and management representatives plus three academic specialists in industrial relations. A good part of the service provided by ACAS used to be rendered by the Department of Employment, but therein it became so associated with the implementation of the former Conservative government's incomes policies that it lost its credibility with the labour movement as an impartial dispute settling agency. Consequently when the Labour Party was returned to office it was decided to combine the effected services within the Department of Employment with some of those of the former Commission on Industrial Relations which was then in the process of being abolished. The result was the formation of ACAS as a multi-purpose body which provides a variety of services ranging from arbitration and conciliation and mediation, through investigatory reports on troublesome industrial relations situations, to the preparation of codes of industrial practice under a number of statutes calling for such codes.

What is especially intriguing about the governance of ACAS is that it involves labour and management in the administration of a tribunal which determines many of the rules and regulations under which they must jointly operate. In addition it tends to ensure the availability of mutually satisfactory dispute intervention machinery because the parties themselves are responsible for the provision of this machinery.

DEVELOPMENTS IN OTHER COUNTRIES

Many other examples of joint or multipartite management of selected public programs are to be found in different Western European countries. In at least one country — Belgium — one can even find some social security systems that are administered by one or the other party; although normally in accordance with statutory provisions and under the scrutiny of advisory and consultative committees involving other interested groups. Thus, in the case of unemployment insurance for unionized workers, the benefits are paid out by their unions; whereas the national holiday pay plan is administered by the employers.

In the Netherlands, in contrast, labour and management are jointly responsible for the administration of most social security programs relating to work. These are known as employed persons' insurance schemes and include unemployment insurance and workmen's compensation. When it comes to national or public insurance schemes, such as family allowances and orphans' and widows' benefits, labour and management at best play only an advisory and consultative role. Overseeing the combination of private and public social security systems which operates in the Netherlands is a tripartite Social Security Council which monitors what is going on in the entire sphere. It is also interesting to note that the country's Social and Economic Council is undertaking a study of the country's confusing mixture of public, branch or industry, and enterprise pension plans with a view to the development of one comprehensive national plan.

France is another country where, despite relatively little headway in many other areas of industrial democracy, much progress has been made in terms of labour and management involvement in the administration of a wide range of social security programs. In this respect France represents a sharp contrast to Italy, where there seems to be little or no participation by unions and employers in what must be described as a basically inadequate and uneven social security system.

As usual Austria is again somewhat unique in its approach. Although labour and management are formally and legally limited to an advisory and consultative capacity in the case of most manpower and social security systems, when they agree their counsel appears to be tantamount to joint administration given the general corporate nature of decision-making in the country.

CONCLUSION

Joint labour-management and different more multipartite combinations for administering selected public programs have a fairly long and extensive history in a few Western European countries and are showing signs of spreading both within them and to others. There is much to be said for such approaches, if only to place the responsibility for such programs on those who stand to gain or lose the most from them. Although there have been some signs of resistance within government bureaucracies to the transfer of power over any of their domains, this has yet to prove an insurmountable obstacle where unions and employers have shown any real desire to assume more joint jurisdiction over systems that should be of even greater mutual concern to them than to government.

Chapter 7

WORKER REPRESENTATION ON COMPANY BOARDS

There is no more central or contentious issue today in the ongoing debate about industrial democracy in Western Europe than the question of worker representation on company boards. The proponents of such representation perceive it as leading to varying degrees of codecision-making and hence as a logical extension of whatever collective bargaining and information and consultation rights workers enjoy at other levels of industrial democracy. To some of its exponents this type of codetermination in its most advanced forms represents the ultimate in industrial democracy in the enterprise.

Not surprisingly there are wide-ranging viewpoints on this subject among both unions and employers. There is considerable ambivalence on the side of organized labour. Unions desire, on the one hand, to be represented on enterprise decision-making bodies; but fear, on the other hand, that they or their members may be coopted by or integrated into the capitalist and/or individual company system. Employers vary in their reaction to this form of industrial democracy from hostility, opposition and rejection to cautious and sometimes even positive acceptance of the concept, if only to the extent of minority worker representation. The spectrum of attitudes on both sides of the issue is naturally much more complex than this brief summary or even the remainder of this chapter can convey. Regardless of this spread in positions the trend is now clearly in the direction of more worker representation on all types of company boards.

Given the controversial and topical nature of the subject of this chapter, it is organized in a manner which requires some explanation. It begins by trying to get at both the real and the superficial differences between unitary and two-tier company boards. After that some of the major developments throughout Western Europe in the area of worker representation on company boards are reviewed. Although this country by country review brings out many of the issues involved in this form of industrial democracy, it seems appropriate to gather many of these issues together for a series of brief critical analyses towards the end of the chapter.

Virtually ignored throughout the chapter are long-standing worker representation systems on the boards of nationalized firms and industries and other public undertakings, where the form of employee participation involved may be quite similar or dissimilar to that in the private sector of the economy. The reason for this omission is partly due to the less contentious nature of some of the problems raised, especially those growing out of such emotional questions as confidentiality of information and property rights. In addition, such bodies are often circumscribed in many fields — including such critical areas as their investment strategies and sometimes even their industrial relations and personnel practices — by government policies reflecting broader political considerations.

UNITARY AND TWO-TIER COMPANY BOARDS: A DISTINCTION OF VARYING SIGNIFICANCE

At the outset it is important to try to delineate the pertinent distinctions between unitary and two-tier company boards, since the implications of worker representation on such boards may vary considerably depending upon the type of board in question. This is not an easy task, as the differences between unitary and two-tier boards can all too readily be either exaggerated or minimized. Superficially it may appear that a unitary board concentrates all decision-making power in one body — conventionally termed a board of directors — while a two-tier board entails varying divisions of this power between what in Germany and a few other countries are termed a supervisory board and a management board. The problem is that it is not this straightforward.

Both types of board arrangements do tend to share one thing in common, but after that it becomes difficult to generalize. Traditionally what they have both had to recognize is their ultimate responsibility to the enterprise shareholders in the form of their annual company meeting or its equivalent. Even this primary responsibility is being increasingly questioned in some quarters because of the alleged inability of an often diffused and large body of shareholders with limited expertise to exercise effective control over the directors of the enterprise they collectively own. Adding to this concern in some instances is the domination by company boards of executive or inside directors as distinct from non-executive or outside directors, and a tendency by such boards to delegate more and more of their effective decision-making to powerful subcommittees which in turn may be even more dominated by the company's top management. Later on it will also be seen that the supposed ultimate control of shareholders is also being diluted or watered down by having corporations or enterprises assume wider responsibilities, both to their employees and to the public at large. Whatever the ultimate responsibilities of company boards, the differences between their unitary and two-tier versions are sometimes very real and sometimes not so real.

Between shareholders' meetings unitary boards are legally the supreme decision-making bodies in their enterprises. But what this means in practice varies immensely. Some boards of directors meet regularly, have active subcommittees and keep a close watch over their company's affairs. Other boards meet only as often as required by law, and then rather perfunctorily, and only exercise general supervisory powers over the management of the company. Still others are even less responsible and more or less accept what the top executive officers of the firm propose until something goes wrong. At least when it comes to day-to-day management and relatively minor policy decisions most companies with unitary boards rely on executive or management committees which report to the board. Often this committee is entirely composed of, or at least clearly dominated by, the company's senior executives. Such executives, in one way or another, usually exercise a great deal of influence over the board of directors. They often end up operating the company essentially on their own. This tendency is reinforced when boards of directors are themselves composed of a majority of executive or inside, as distinct from non-executive or outside, members.

It is at this point that the difference between a unitary and two-tier board arrangement can become very subtle and superficial, if not non-existent. A unitary board usually names the members of a firm's executive or general management committee, where there is one, and the chief executive officers, whether there is such a committee or not. The supervisory board under a two-tier system names the members of the management board, if not other senior executive officers as well. This management board and these senior executive officers are responsible for directing and managing the company under the overall policy guidance and general scrutiny of the supervisory board. Once appointed, the management board and senior executives can become a sufficient force unto themselves to keep the supervisory board from exercising too much supervision over them. Many a supervisory board is realistically limited to accepting or vetoing the action of its management board. Moreover, if the latter is challenged by the supervisory board, it can in some countries appeal to a shareholders' meeting to resolve the matter in its favour.

Neither unitary boards nor supervisory boards in two-tier setups are normally equipped to take on the senior operating managers of a company unless it is in some difficulty. Even then the more direct and immediate experience and acquired expertise which the key executives have available to them puts them at a natural advantage. The fact that under both systems the senior managers almost invariably attend the top board meetings in one capacity or another adds to their ability to dominate the scene, until something goes so obviously astray in the conduct of the enterprise that they have to be called to account.

Lest the impression be left that there is no major difference between a unitary and two-tier board system, the two extreme ends of the spectrum should be highlighted to reveal just how far apart they can become in practice. At one end of the spectrum there are still to be found unitary boards where the majority, if not all of the members, are drawn from the ranks of the company's full-time senior executives. Such a board is quite indistinguishable from the top management of the company, since it is, in fact, composed of precisely that group of individuals. At the other end of the spectrum are supervisory boards under two-tier systems where none of the members are full-time company officers. The potential room for division and friction with the key operating personnel of the enterprise is then much more marked. This potential can be great enough when all such board members are themselves shareholders or shareholder nominees. It can be magnified greatly when other types of representatives — such as those of the work force or the public in general — are added.

The more the potential for lack of unanimity between any kind of company board and top management, the more inclined the latter is to favour a two-tier board. This is based on the supposition that supervisory boards are much less likely to exercise detailed supervision over management. While there is considerable evidence to support this point of view, it does not necessarily follow that, in practice, supervisory boards behave that much differently than unitary boards when it comes to overseeing the top executive's performance.

Once worker representation on company boards becomes a very real prospect management reaction to whether it would prefer such representation on a unitary or supervisory board really depends on the way the board or boards they have known function. Correspondingly union thinking on the subject is increasingly influenced by the same type of experience. Perhaps, when all is said and done, the point to be stressed above all is that forms and names may not count for all that much, since unitary and supervisory boards can behave both among and between themselves either quite differently or very similarly.

CODETERMINATION IN WEST GERMANY

The idea of worker representation on company supervisory boards has a long history in West Germany. It was first introduced under the Works Council Act of 1920 which authorized works councils to nominate two such representatives. Like all other forms of industrial democracy in West Germany this concept disappeared during the Nazi regime, only to be reborn again after the war. At that time it initially reappeared in the Montan or coal and steel industry where it was favoured by the unions and the British occupying authorities and accepted by the employers, if only as an alternative to the permanent expropriation which some of them feared. Since then in West Germany there has been an unending stream of debates and developments concerning codetermination. As a result it now takes such a range of forms in different settings that it is difficult to keep each of their major features straight, let alone their immensely detailed application.

The Montan or Coal and Steel Model

The most advanced or radical form of codetermination in West Germany is still to be found in the Montan or coal and steel industry. Introduced in 1948, and now operating under the Codetermination Act of 1951, this version of codetermination provides workers with the same number of representatives on the company boards as the shareholders. This parity model has a few other special features which do not show up at all, or to a lesser extent, in the other models surveyed below. On the worker side, for example, two representatives are selected by the company's elected works council from among its own ranks or the work force as a whole. Normally these are the chairman and vice-chairman of the works council. To ensure a more direct union voice at the board level two more worker representatives are selected by the union after consultation with the works council. Another worker representative is selected by the West German Federation of Labour (the DGB) from outside the ranks of the unions and workers involved. One of the representatives on each of the workers' and shareholders' halves of the board — the latter one in the case of the workers' half — must not be either a worker or shareholder or have any other interest in the company or union in question. All these members together are then supposed to select an independent and neutral chairman. In the event of serious difficulty in choosing such an individual a special form of conciliation is called into play. The general meeting of the shareholders makes the final choice if this procedure, as well as a possible appeal mechanism involving the civil courts, fails to resolve the impasse. Such an impasse seldom, if ever, seems to have occurred.

Another striking feature of this parity model of codetermination relates to the means by which a specially designated labour director is chosen as one of the three-man management board. Besides a labour director there is usually also a financial and a technical director on the management board. While all three members of the management board must be approved by a majority of the total supervisory board, the labour director must not only meet this test but also be acceptable to a majority of the worker representatives alone. Almost invariably this means that the labour director is drawn from a list of union and works council chosen candidates which usually includes active and former union representatives as well as more independent individuals known for their understanding of labour's point of view.

Such labour directors are normally responsible for industrial relations, personnel policies and what the West Germans and most Western Europeans call social policies. The latter may embrace everything from cafeterias and day-care centres to housing and recreational facilities. Some of the responsibilities borne by labour directors are of a critical and sensitive nature from management's point of view. Yet the worker representatives on supervisory boards have in effect veto power over their appointment and reappointment. Conceivably this could subject labour directors to an impossible conflict of interest. This dilemma is minimized insofar as collective bargaining itself is concerned because it is handled at the national or regional level of the industry in a manner which does not necessarily directly involve the individual company labour directors. To the extent that a possible conflict of interest remains within companies in terms of contract administration and other tension-prone areas, a kind of accommodation appears to have been worked out in many companies. Under this accommodation labour directors have been converted into what amounts to a form of conciliator or mediator between the union and works council representatives and their colleagues on the management board and in the managerial hierarchy in general. This is hardly unique to West Germany or to its special parity codetermination model. Many a vice president or director of industrial relations in North America frequently finds himself playing a roughly similar role, although hardly under the same confines and constraints. The novel labour director aspect of the coal and steel parity model has not been extended by law in its totality to any other version of codetermination in West Germany to date. Although a variation on the same idea has been introduced into the new compromise codetermination law which could have the same effect in practice.

The New Compromise Codetermination Law

The West German labour movement has fought for about three decades to have the Montan or coal and steel model of codetermination extended throughout all major enterprises in the country. Management has resisted this proposal just as strongly as the unions have promoted it. Recently a complex compromise on this vexing question was arrived at between the political parties in the country — a compromise which for different reasons has not satisfied any of the major interest groups embroiled in the struggle over the issue, except perhaps for the coal and steel unions and workers whose model was left intact.

The new model embodied in the Codetermination Act of 1976 which applies to firms with over 2000 employees appears, on the surface, to grant workers parity with shareholders on supervisory boards. It probably does not really do so in fact for two reasons. For one thing, one of the worker representatives is to be chosen from among the managerial personnel. Furthermore, the supervisory board chairman, who cannot be appointed against the wishes of the shareholder representatives on the board, has a double vote if for any reason there is a need for such a vote to resolve a deadlock on the board.

Beyond the issue of whether or not the new model does or does not involve parity of workers and shareholders there are a host of other complications in the new procedures for selecting the worker representatives on the boards. These new procedures, for the most part, seem to dilute the direct role of unions in this process. The proportion of union officials on the workers' half of the board is reduced and they must be elected either directly or indirectly through a college or series of colleges of electors by the work force as a whole from among a required minimum number of nominees put forward by the unions. As for the rest of the electoral rules and regulations they defy accurate and brief description. Their overall intent, on balance, seems to be to ensure that the workers have a greater voice in determining who their representatives are to be. Thus, just as the unions must submit their candidates to an election by all workers in the enterprise to decide which union nominees are to represent them, so the executive or managerial official who sits on the board must be elected by a constituency which includes all the salaried staff — even though the minimal requirement of two management nominees must originate with and come from among the executive and managerial staff.

The chairman and deputy chairman of supervisory boards under this new complex compromise system must both be elected by two-thirds majorities on the boards. If these majorities cannot be obtained the shareholder members choose the chairman, who has that critical double vote in the event of an impasse on the board, and the worker members decide on the deputy chairman. The entire board selects the members of the management board, again on the basis of a two-thirds majority. If this majority does not materialize a mediation procedure comes into operation, and if that fails to solve the problem the chairman of the supervisory board ends up deciding the matter.

Two other divergences from the Montan parity model should also be noted in passing. The first concerns the position of the labour director. Although such a position with a similar jurisdiction is made mandatory in all the affected firms, the encumbent is not to be subject to a veto power by the worker representatives on the supervisory board. This means he or she will be appointed and reappointed by the same means as the other two members of the management board — that is by a two-thirds overall majority on the supervisory board. Should the labour director lose the confidence or incur the wrath of the workers' representatives, this may be small consolation because he or she probably would not be reappointed then in any event. It is also noteworthy that the new law requires that all three groups of workers in a company — that is, shop floor, staff, and executive or managerial — be represented proportionately on the supervisory board, subject to the proviso that there be a minimum of at least one representative from each group. This can make a real difference in the type of union and works council nominees put forward and elected to the boards, where organized labour is weak among any segment of a company's work force.

The One-Third Model of Codetermination

All but family-owned companies with less than 500 employees which are not covered by the aforementioned versions of codetermination are governed by the minority or one-third model promulgated under the Works Constitution Act of 1952. Formerly applying to all but the Montan or coal and steel industry, this model of codetermination provides for a direct and secret ballot election by the employees of a company of one-third of its supervisory board. Accordingly, it entails no assured union presence as such on the board; although the electoral process usually leads to such a situation in all highly organized firms. Although employers in general grew to accept this form of codetermination, the labour movement resisted it from the outset because of the minority position of the worker representatives and the lack of any direct role in their selection by the unions.

An Overall Appraisal

Codetermination thus far seems to have served West Germany well. This overall assessment was borne out by the findings of the Biedenkopf Committee — a fairly representative committee composed of a reasonably balanced membership — which reported in 1970 after an exhaustive inquiry into the functioning of the system. Nonetheless the system does have its detractors. The most vociferous detractors tend to come from the extreme left and right wings of the political sphere. These people share the ideological and philosophical stance that codetermination represents at least a form of cooptation and integration, if not complete sellout of their two respective points of view. The far left and the far right draw intriguingly contrary conclusions about where codetermination will ultimately lead. The former fear that it will lessen the prospects for the fundamental transformation of society they favour, while the latter are concerned that it will undermine the existing capitalistic or enterprise system. The latter view is now quite widely shared among a broad spectrum of employers as a result of the recent codetermination extensions. Codetermination also has its more pragmatic critics. Many employers criticize the compromises, delays and politics involved; while some trade unionists will settle for nothing less than parity on supervisory boards with increased scope to exercise more scrutiny over the management conduct of an enterprise's affairs.

In terms of its actual effect on company decision-making, codetermination has first of all usually led to much more active and informed board level deliberations. Beyond this effect it appears to have had a much greater impact on areas of immediate concern to workers than on broader policy matters. Even in the Montan or coal and steel full parity model, management still appears comparatively free to conduct an enterprise's overall business in accordance with its own best judgement, provided this has no harmful side effects on the work force. Such side effects tend to be minimized insofar as possible by management's heightened sensitivity to them, a change that has been clearly brought about largely by codetermination.

Worker representatives on company boards have a great deal of influence, if not a decisive voice, when it comes to taking into consideration the human variable in board level decisions. Such representatives seem, for the most part, to have been content with this degree of control over the situation to date. Although they participate in the debates and discussions involving general financial, marketing and production issues it is only when they envisage some serious consequence for the labour force that they tend to challenge management proposals.

Referring to the Montan or full parity model, the aforementioned Biedenkopf Report found some signs of compromises and delays but little evidence of stalemates. This is because management is usually careful in areas affecting the work force to clear its plans with the unions and/or works councils before they become an issue at the board level. The explanation in other areas normally lies in the worker representatives' acceptance or acquiescence in management's proposals, if only because of insufficient expertise on their part to question seriously management's judgements. Moreover, the worker representatives are usually as interested in the company's welfare as the shareholders. The Biedenkopf Report concluded, in general, that codetermination was working quite well in the sense of having no major adverse effects on company efficiency.

There are at least two major risks or threats to Germany's codetermination system in the long run. One is the possibility of a mixture of apathy, complacency and alienation among workers overcoming the whole structure if too much elitism and formalism, as described in a later section of this chapter, envelops the process. The other risk or threat lies in the conceivable dependence of the entire West German socio-economic-political system on prosperity. The very stability of West Germany may hinge on the ability to continue to generate relatively rapid rises in its workers' standard of living. Given its unavoidable reliance on exports for its manufactured goods and even heavier reliance on imports for its energy requirements and raw materials, the country and its prosperity are exposed and vulnerable to many forces beyond its control.

The point should be added to these broad speculative concerns that it will take time to assess the effect of the new compromise model of codetermination. Hopefully the results of this new model will be monitored more carefully and continually than the overall results of codetermination to date. One of the reasons why there is so much undocumented conjecture about the entire system is that so little penetrating analysis has been undertaken into its operation, aside from the now somewhat dated Biedenkopf Report.

A final word of caution is in order about the West German experience with codetermination. Although this point is made repeatedly throughout this volume about every form of industrial democracy in different countries, it must be underscored at this point. Just because some forms of codetermination have served West Germany well does not mean that they would have the same effect elsewhere. West Germany has at least two major advantages when it comes to codetermination. The first of these lies in the self-discipline of its people and work force. Nowhere in Western Europe is the work ethic more alive and well than in West Germany. The country also benefits from the most rationally organized labour movement in any of the countries surveyed. Basically there is one industrial union for every major industry. Although these two advantages may not be essential to the effective operation of a codetermination system, they certainly raise the prospects for its success.

THE NETHERLANDS VERSION — A CASE OF MUTUAL VETO RIGHTS

Since 1973 major corporate boards in the Netherlands have been engaged in the process of phasing in a novel compromise proposal on codetermination arrived at unanimously in its Social and Economic Council. The Council strongly endorsed worker participation in the selection of company board members, but rejected the idea of direct union and/or worker representation — as well as that of managers or shareholders — on the grounds that this could lead to an unworkable combination of both conflicts of interest and factionalism.

Instead of anything like the West German approach, the Netherlands devised a system under which supervisory boards coopt new members who are acceptable to both employee and shareholder interests. As well as one of mutual veto rights this system may be described as mutual cooptation. Nominations for new board members may come from the supervisory board itself, the management board, the enterprise or works council, or the shareholders' meeting. No such nominee can be a shareholder or be in the employ of either the company or the union or unions representing its employees. The supervisory board makes the final selection, but not before notifying the works council and shareholders' meeting.

Either one of the latter may object to the proposed appointment on one of two grounds. The first is that the individual in question is simply not qualified to sit on the supervisory board. The second and potentially more significant objection may be based on the question of balance within the board. It is at this point that the situation in the Netherlands becomes more difficult to explain. Although the law does not require parity of employee and shareholder interests — let alone representation — on company boards, it does imply an underlying thrust at least to the former effect. Thus, in their final selection of new members to join their ranks, supervisory boards must clearly bear in mind a reasonable balance of employee and shareholder interests. More often than not the working out of this equation also takes into consideration some element of the public interest, in the form of completely independent or neutral members.

In the event of a disagreement between the supervisory board and either the shareholders' meeting or the works council about proposed new members of the board, the matter may be referred to the Social and Economic Council by the board. The Council may either uphold the latter's judgement or order it to start its selection procedure all over again. So far there have been few such referrals, which seems to indicate that consultation among the various interests involved usually ensures an appropriate mix of new supervisory board members as openings for them occur. One can only imagine the compromising, politicking and trading-off that must sometimes take place in this process.

Despite some such difficulties, most of the affected enterprises in the Netherlands seem to have accommodated themselves to the new system for board member selection, and it appears to be working out in many firms. The problem is that while management has come to accept the new system, the unions and their political allies are now demanding direct West German-style worker representation on company boards. Both groups are divided in terms of the proportions of worker representation they favour and in terms of the question of whether there should be any public representation. Organized labour's criticism of the present Netherlands system seems to be largely based on their purported lack of power over those they agree to on the boards, as well as what they claim are inadequate reporting back procedures.

Management in the Netherlands is opposed to any basic change in the present system and takes exception to the union criticism of it. Employers point out, referring to the related issues of control and feedback, that the works councils not only have veto power over initial appointments to the boards but on reappointments to which each board member is subject every four years. Also, the board, or part thereof, must meet with the works council at least twice a year to review the general company outlook. Under proposed new legislation pertaining to works councils, boards will have to meet with them on any planned changes of major consequence. Works councils will also be able to call for outside investigations of a company's affairs when they have grounds for serious concern about management's conduct of the business.

Regardless of the merits of the case, it seems likely that the Netherlands will revise its policy on codetermination within the next year or so to include appointed or elected worker representatives on company boards. What appears most likely is some variation on one of the EEC models discussed later in this chapter incorporating some neutral or public as well as labour and management representation.

BRITAIN'S BULLOCK REPORT

One of the early parts of Britain's lingering social contract between the labour movement and the labour party called upon the latter to introduce some form of industrial democracy into British industry. Upon its return to office in 1974, the labour party announced its intention of placing worker representatives on company boards and established the Bullock Commission to determine how best to proceed with this objective.

The first point to be made about the Bullock Commission is that it did not represent an impartial inquiry into the principles of industrial democracy in general or codetermination in particular as they might or might not suit the British situation. Politically the matter of principle was already settled as far as the government was concerned. This decision was openly reflected in the Commission's terms of reference, which made it clear that its main task was to ascertain how best to proceed with codetermination along lines satisfactory to the Trade Union Congress. Given these terms of reference, only those prepared in advance to accept the principle of codetermination could serve on the Commission. As a result, its composition ended up almost as loaded as its circumscribed mandate. With one or two exceptions, the Commission was composed of enthusiastic trade union proponents of codetermination, reluctant but somewhat supportive industrialists and frankly sympathetic academics.

Given a one year period in which to report, the Commission undertook little research, briefly visited only Germany and Sweden, and accepted oral evidence solely from a small and carefully selected group of individuals and institutions. It is quite ironic, to say the least, that a Commission, charged with determining the best way to introduce one of the cornerstones of industrial democracy in the corporate sphere, should have conducted its own business in such a contrary spirit. Because of its terms of reference, its composition, the way in which it proceeded and the many media leaks about the directions of its split thinking, there were few surprises when the Report of the Commission was released.

Succinctly stated, the predictable majority of the Bullock Commission came out strongly for parity of worker with shareholder representation on the conventional British unitary board of directors, with all of the worker representatives to be chosen by the union officials and shop stewards in the enterprise in question. Parity, as distinct from minority worker representation, was recommended primarily on the grounds that workers could not be held equally accountable with management for a firm's performance, unless they had an equal voice in its operation. Should parity of employee and shareholder representation ever give rise to stalemates, provision was made for a smaller third element to be chosen jointly by the larger employee and shareholder representatives or by a quasi-public Industrial Democracy Commission if they could not agree among themselves. This Bullock majority proposal for the composition of company boards became known as the $2X + Y$ formula.

Continuation of the traditional unitary British board under codetermination was urged for several reasons. For one thing it was held that there would be immense legal and practical problems involved in converting British companies from one- to two-tier board operations. The more deeply rooted reason for this position appears to have been the feeling that unitary boards are far more influential in the management of firms than are supervisory boards. Given that the majority of the Commission envisaged codetermination in large measure as an extension of collective bargaining, it wanted to ensure that the worker representatives were sitting on the decisive decision-making body in the enterprise.

The latter rationale also serves to explain why the majority came out strongly for a single union instead of a dual union-worker or worker channel for selecting the employee representatives on company boards. After all, if codetermination is envisaged largely if not primarily as an extension of collective bargaining, then it is crucial that the union or unions which represent the workers in collective bargaining should also control their representatives in the codetermination sphere. To this end the majority suggested that Employee Representative Committees, composed of the union officials and shop stewards in each enterprise, be constituted to name the worker representatives on its board.

Although the minority on the Bullock Commission accepted the principle of codetermination — they really had no choice if they were going to sit on the Commission — they parted company with the majority on all but one of its key proposals. The one exception was parity of employee and shareholder representation, although the minority would couple this with one-third public representation along the lines of one of the EEC models discussed below. Despite the legal and practical problems involved in a changeover, the minority would only apply this system to German-type supervisory boards rather than the customary British unitary boards. The minority also diverged from the majority in holding out for employee-elected, as distinct from union-appointed, worker representatives.

This brief survey of the major differences between the majority and the minority in the Bullock Commission does not begin to do justice to the many related issues it dealt with. Many of these will emerge in later parts of this chapter, as well as in later chapters. The important point to note, for the moment, is that because of and/or despite the heated, and at times, passionate debate it provoked, the Bullock Report has helped to develop more impetus behind the drive for some forms of codetermination in Britain and Western Europe in general. It will have this effect if only by serving as a catalyst for further discussion, which is about all it deserves to do, given the way it was conceived and conducted.

Except as part of the general political machinations which lie behind the social contract, it is hard to understand the conclusions of the Bullock majority. Although those involved deny it, they are really trying to transplant into Britain virtually overnight a more radical version of West Germany's codetermination than the West Germans have been able to evolve after decades of experience. Already, and again later on, the importance of attitudes and institutions will be emphasized more than anything else when it comes to the advisability and feasibility of attempting such transplants. Britain and West Germany are so different, in both respects, in the field of industrial relations that it is hard to imagine adaptions, let alone imitations, of one country's system working well in the other's without a great deal of caution, nurturing and time.

As for the future of the Bullock Report and codetermination in Britain it is too early to be certain what will happen. In all probability the majority position is not on — as the British would say — for the time being. Almost half the labour movement is still ambivalent about, or quite opposed to, anything like full codetermination. Corporate and management interests are unalterably opposed to anything like parity of employee representation with that of shareholders. Even some elements in the Labour Party government itself now seem concerned about the lengths to which the Bullock majority would go, at least in the private sector of the economy.

The first major codetermination breakthroughs in Britain are coming in the public sector. Led by the Post Office, one is likely to see a succession of experiments with varying degrees of codetermination lying somewhere between the Bullock majority and minority reports. How far these experiments go and how fast they spread to the private sector depends on the broader political forces that are at play in the country, as the Labour Party fights to hold office by retaining the support of the marginal, but now critical, Liberal Party. As in so many other countries in Western Europe, the merits of the case for and against codetermination in British industry could easily become lost in the political shuffle that has and will continue to surround the issue.

DEVELOPMENTS IN OTHER COUNTRIES

Codetermination is in various stages of development in other Western European countries. Little or no movement toward codetermination is taking place in some countries such as Belgium and Italy at present. This is because of a mixture of lack of unified union commitment to the proposition and little government interest in it. The Sudreau Report in France has recommended some changes in the arrangement which has prevailed since 1945 — under which enterprise committees or work councils are allowed two observers on the supervisory boards of companies where they have a voice but not a vote. The number of such observers was doubled in 1972. One was added to represent foremen and other first-line supervisory personnel and another to represent more senior supervisory and technical and professional staff members. The Sudreau Report, which preferred the term co-supervision or co-surveillance to codetermination, recommended that the West German minority or one-third model of worker representation be phased into large French companies as part of a series of proposals to promote more industrial democracy in the country. Although this recommendation appears to be favoured by the government, it is still being widely debated and has yet to be acted upon.

Austria now has the West German minority or one-third model of codetermination in all major enterprises. Austrian labour appears to be quite satisfied with this status for a number of interrelated reasons. In the first place, many Austrian enterprises are government owned and have supervisory boards composed of appointees of the major political parties as well as the workers. Together with their social democratic allies on these boards, this means that the worker representatives can often exercise a decisive influence. Much more will be said about this approach in a later chapter on the future of labour and management. Austrian labour is also extremely well organized both for collective bargaining and for political action. Overall it seems to have developed such a potent combination of other influence-wielding mechanisms that minority or one-third representation on enterprise boards is all that it requires at that level of decision-making, at least in the nationalized industries. It could decide to press for more representation on private company boards, but even this appears unlikely at the present time.

The Scandinavian countries by themselves demonstrate a wide range of developments in the field of codetermination. Finland has only reached the early discussion or preliminary proposal stage in this or any other area of industrial democracy. Denmark now provides for at least two elected worker representatives on company boards, and is also experimenting with public representatives on the boards of banks. But the law still provides that a majority of the members of these boards must be shareholder representatives. Norway has been following its usual tradition of experimentation by trying a variety of codetermination approaches. Recently this experimentation led to a law creating a Board of Representatives or Corporate Assembly for all manufacturing and mining firms with over two hundred employees. Elected workers have one-third of the seats on these boards, which both elect the unitary boards of directors on which the workers may insist on one-third representation and have the final say on all major investments, rationalizations and reorganizations.

Sweden currently represents an especially interesting case in the area of codetermination. Unions have had the right since 1972 to appoint two representatives on major company boards in all but one or two industries. For the moment the labour movement seems to be content with this status, since they construe board representation primarily as a means of securing information and insight about a company and not for anything like codecision-making. Their ambivalence on the latter score is underlined by the fact that some of the public service unions have recently withdrawn from their modified versions of codetermination in the public service — which might better be termed personnel codetermination — in part because they felt it subjected them to an impossible conflict of interest.

Even more significant in the latter decision and in the broader context of codetermination in general in Sweden is the new democracy-at-work legislation. This provides both private and public sector unions with much greater opportunities to press for all manner of codetermination, industrial democracy or joint regulation arrangements at all levels of the undertaking through collective bargaining. As indicated earlier in this volume, this legislation has only recently been enacted and it will take some time for the unions to realize their full potential under it. Also to be stressed is the proposed Meidner plan for worker asset or capital formation which is discussed in a subsequent chapter. One of the eventual and ultimate purposes of this plan is to introduce a form of collective union and worker ownership and control over all Swedish firms.

Where all these interconnected crosscurrents in Sweden will lead is impossible to say, but regardless of how they achieve it one can be sure Swedish labour will eventually have a major, if not equal, voice in enterprise decision-making. As just suggested their chosen route to this end, above and beyond the prospects for the Meidner plan, is currently more likely to be via greatly broadened collective bargaining rights rather than any standardized statutory formula for codetermination.

THE ROLE OF THE EUROPEAN ECONOMIC COMMISSION

The role of the EEC in promoting various forms of industrial democracy was emphasized in an earlier chapter. At this point the purpose is to review the two primary vehicles by which it is attempting to achieve this purpose at the company board level. One is on the inter-country front and involves the proposed board structure for companies which choose to incorporate on a European wide basis. The other is the proposed Fifth Directive on European company law, which is designed to harmonize some of the key features of such laws within each of the member countries.

The proposed European Companies Statute is intended to encourage the maximum advantages to be derived by enterprises operating throughout the Common Market by permitting them to incorporate on a similar basis. This would solve many of the complex, expensive and inefficient legal and practical problems associated with the current state-by-state incorporation of multinational corporations functioning through all kinds of subsidiaries, thereby facilitating greater economies of scale and other advantages. In return for the resulting benefits and privileges afforded such companies, and as part of the general EEC push for greater industrial democracy, the proposed European Companies Statute would require these companies to accept more employee participation in their decision-making bodies at a number of levels and in a number of ways. Aside from providing for European-wide collective agreements and European-wide works councils (the latter are discussed in the next chapter), the latest version of the Statute requires that the employees and the shareholders each elect one third of the supervisory board members and then together coopt the other third to represent general interests independent of both employee and shareholder concerns. How far and fast this proposed statute moves forward depends on developments surrounding the Fifth Directive. The European Companies Statute can neither be too much more conservative than the former (or companies will resort to it to escape more onerous national requirements for worker participation) nor much more radical than the former (or no firms will take advantage of it.)

Under the proposed Fifth Directive on the structure of public companies, member states are currently to be offered a choice as to the procedure they follow to provide for employee participation in the selection of supervisory board members. Essentially the member states would have to choose between a variation on the West German minority one-third model of directly elected worker representatives and a version of the Dutch mutual-veto model, entailing cooptation of a mixture of new board members mutually satisfactory to both the employees and the shareholders. If operating under the latter model, member states would also be empowered to insist on some degree of public representation on company boards if they so desired.

The proposed Fifth Directive is now being reassessed in the light of ongoing developments in the member states. While some, like Belgium and Italy, have made little progress in this area, West Germany has gone well beyond the proposed Fifth Directive with its new compromise model of codetermination, and the Bullock Commission has come up with an even more advanced or radical version for Britain. The challenge of reconciling all these heterogeneous approaches is difficult, to say the least. Yet the EEC does not seem disposed to ease up on its goal of reducing what it believes are unacceptably high degrees of divergence between the mechanisms and practices of employee participation in corporate decision-making in different countries. Rather it is likely to push even harder for a reduction in these divergences, but do so in a more flexible manner and with greater allowance for the transitional problems which some countries are bound to experience. Even this more pragmatic and realistic approach may take years before it yields any concrete legislative results at the community level, let alone in some of the countries which seem most reluctant to move on this front.

CONTINUING ISSUES AND PROBLEMS

From among and between the codetermination developments within the EEC and individual Western European countries, there emerge a wide range of continuing issues and problems, some of which bear special mention at this point. Some issues, such as those concerning information and confidentiality and education and training, are left to a later chapter. Others have already been dealt with adequately or will surface in the concluding chapter.

The Ideological Spread in Viewpoints

Although the wide gulf in thinking about the principles involved in codetermination has been touched upon at many points previously, it has to be underscored again at this point because of its potential impact upon further developments in this field. Despite the gradual convergence of thinking which appears to be taking place, there are still many sharp differences of opinion. Many employers, on the one hand, continue to resist any more radical forms of codetermination than they are compelled to absorb by law. Even then some of them at best accept only the letter of the law and not its spirit. On the other hand, the extreme left wing of the labour movement, as well as some of its social democratic components, remains highly skeptical of, if not totally hostile to, any form of involvement in management decision-making. This attitude reflects concern about anything which could compromise the independence and integrity of the labour movement as a force for the radical reform or transformation of society.

This broad spectrum of viewpoints about codetermination not only serves to delay more movement in the area, but also to aggravate many of the other issues and problems that surround the concept. Were it not for these extreme divisions of opinion it might be easier to resolve some of these other difficulties. At the same time it must be recognized that some of these difficulties are in themselves so deep-seated that they do not lend themselves to any easy or ready solutions.

Delays, Compromises and Politics

As a later chapter will reveal even more pointedly than this one has, one of management's primary complaints about codetermination concerns the delays, compromises and politics it can introduce into the corporate decision-making process. That this is not an imaginary worry is borne out by the increasing number of conciliation and adjudication mechanisms which are being built into some of the more advanced codetermination systems in order to break potential deadlocks. Sometimes this machinery is available solely to deal with splits over those who should be selected to serve as members or chairpersons of company boards. In other cases, both at the board and works council levels, such machinery has been evolved to cope with more substantive differences, such as the provisions which should be introduced to cope with the human adjustments made necessary by major industrial conversions.

It is a fact of industrial relations life that all forms of industrial democracy — including the most traditional forms of North American style collective bargaining — often slow down management decision-making procedures. In and of itself, this may seem deleterious on a number of grounds. But it may also be that the delays, compromises and politics which are involved lead to better, or at least more readily implementable, decisions. This is a matter which warrants and will receive more thorough attention in a subsequent chapter.

Union and Worker Conflicts of Interest

A concern shared by many labour as well as management representatives is that union and worker representatives on company boards will be confronted by serious conflicts of interest. The degree of this risk hinges in part on how the responsibilities of such representatives are defined — a matter dealt with later on in this chapter. It also depends in part on the nature of the boards' functions. If these are essentially fairly broad and supervisory in nature then the risks of such conflict are minimized. The more involved boards become in day-to-day and detailed company activities, the greater the possible dilemmas involved.

Concern about the possibility of conflict of interest is particularly pronounced when it comes to collective bargaining. Even in this potentially delicate area the problem may be virtually non-existent, since company boards may not even be involved in the negotiation process except by way of sanctioning the final outcome. If collective bargaining does become a board level issue, one way to solve the difficulty is to follow the Swedish approach of exempting the employee representatives from such deliberations. As opposed to this approach some would argue that it is useful to have some union and worker input, even in these kinds of discussions, if only to ensure that their positions are fully appreciated.

Union and worker representatives, in general, do not appear to have felt subjected to undue conflicts of interest growing out of their board memberships. Many employer spokesmen support this contention, as well as the related point that whatever conflicts of interest may be entailed can often be more than offset by the realistic appraisals of an enterprise's economic and financial situation which union and worker representatives can feed back to their colleagues. The result can be a more reasonable negotiating climate and a correspondingly greater opportunity for achieving a mutually satisfactory agreement.

Unitary or Two-Tier Boards

Until the Bullock Commission reported, the general consensus in Western Europe was clearly to the effect that codetermination should take place on the supervisory level of two-tier company board systems. Whether the Bullock Report will lead to a change in this consensus remains to be seen. For the moment this seems unlikely, since most trade union advocates of codetermination still seem to want to limit their role, and that of worker representatives, to participation in broad policy determination, and to avoid any involvement in the application of policy where they prefer to maintain their complete independence of action and reaction. This approach could change either as the distinction between unitary and two-tier boards becomes more blurred or if, as and when worker representatives on supervisory boards becomes disillusioned with the degree of influence they are able to exercise on such a body.

From a more general point of view the main advantages of a truly dual board level structure is that it permits a combination of pluralistic interest representation in broad policy formulation at the supervisory board level with reasonably harmonious and homogeneous administration at the management board level. This point becomes the more telling as increasing attention is focused on representation of interest groups other than labour and management on company boards.

The Power of Supervisory Boards

The previous set of considerations brings out one of the main reasons why the power of supervisory boards is such a critical matter. Typical of the evolving Western European scene in this respect is the current EEC position. By and large its proposals would make the supervisory board responsible for the appointment, general overseeing and, if and when necessary, the removal of the management board. The supervisory board would also have to be consulted before any major decisions were made which could have adverse effects on the work force. As suggested in an earlier section, such decisions would tend to include major acquisitions, mergers, reorganizations, technological changes and the like. As long as supervisory boards actually have effective control over the selection of management boards and can effectively scrutinize any of their key proposals which are bound to have an impact on the labour force — before they are made, let alone implemented — unions may well remain satisfied with the situation. Otherwise the possible trend of events is quite impossible to predict.

The Proportion of Worker Representatives on Company Boards

Minority versus parity worker representation on supervisory boards will remain a contentious issue for the forseeable future. Almost without exception employers remain adamantly opposed to equality of employee with shareholder representation, even when this is accompanied by a third independent or neutral element. Within the ranks of organized labour, opinion on this issue ranges from the West German trade union demand for complete parity in the name of full codetermination to the Swedish labour movement's current satisfaction with minority representation for information and insight. The problem with parity is that it sets the stage for conflict and confrontation other than in the collective bargaining arena, and compels the injection of some sort of a third element in order to resolve any possible impasses. Parity also invites the ultimate in potential union and worker conflict of interest, short of worker control or self management. In contrast, the difficulty with minority representation lies in the fact that it may amount to little more than a gesture or token if management decides to treat it accordingly or union and worker representatives really feel that it puts them at a distinct disadvantage. On balance, employer-accepted minority representation may well make more sense than parity, even from a union point of view — provided this form of codetermination is part of a totally integrated overall system of industrial democracy, including an effective collective bargaining procedure and other forms of worker representation at lower levels in the enterprise.

Relationship to Other Forms of Industrial Democracy

The importance of the latter point cannot be minimized. If any form of board level codetermination is to be effective from an employee point of view, it must be tied in with other forms of worker representation. Where the work councils involved play a major part in the selection of employee representatives on company boards this is almost invariably the case — as their key officers are normally chosen. Even when the employees elect their representatives on the board the same effect is often ensured, because of the successful slates of candidates put forward by the unions and works councils.

Effective links must be maintained between the various levels and types of employee representation, if those workers who serve on company boards are not to function in something of a vacuum. In that event disillusionment is bound to set in, not only among the other types of employee representatives but also among the work force as a whole. Labour must develop an integrated overall approach to all forms of industrial democracy if the various parts of the system are to yield their full potential.

Degree of Union Control over Worker Representatives

Assuming unions represent the basic instrument for worker representation within an enterprise, it is only natural that the question should arise as to the degree of control they should have over those who serve on company boards on labour's behalf. In all but the West German minority or one-third version of codetermination, provision is made for direct union representation among those who sit as worker representatives on company boards in that country. One criticism of this approach is that employees might prefer a different type of representative than a union official or even a works councillor on the boards of enterprises. A possible way out is provided under the German compromise model which allows the unions alone to nominate a minority of the candidates for the board, but leaves it to the employees to make the final selection. Certainly it seems somewhat inconsistent for organized labour to argue for full control over those who are to represent the workers on enterprise boards, when the whole process is supposed to be in the name of industrial democracy. The risk of leaving the entire selection process in the hands of the employees — which most employers favour because of their fear of entrenched and institutionalized union-management conflict at the board level — not only lies in possible lack of integration with other forms of industrial democracy, but in the development of an unduly high degree of company or enterprise orientation among employee representatives.

This is a potentially serious problem which can occur at the company board or works council level or at any other point in an industrial democracy system. Company or enterprise orientation by worker representatives in its most extreme form can lead to employer-employee collusion. Unions themselves may even become involved in such conspiracies, which can amount to little more than a compact to take advantage of the public. That unions are aware of these risks is best demonstrated by the attitude of the West German labour movement which, in the Montan or coal and steel model of codetermination, favours a mixture of union and worker representatives from within the union and company involved, as well as one from outside their immediate orbit. At the very least, a mixture of union and worker selected representatives would seem to be required to minimize the risks involved. Beyond this position there is the more general question of public representation on company boards, a subject which will be dealt with shortly.

The Responsibility of Worker Representatives

One issue or problem that has been sharpened by the Bullock Report pertains to the legal responsibilities of worker representatives on company boards. Most systems of codetermination have thus far operated on the assumption that worker representatives should bear the same responsibilities as those of their shareholder counterparts. This means that their primary responsibility should be to the interests of the company as a whole and to its owners. Although this has not precluded worker representatives from pressing for more consideration of employee interests, it does tend to constrain them somewhat. For this reason the Bullock Report recommended that all board members bear in mind the interests of employees and shareholders as more or less copartners in enterprises. This is in keeping with the movement of law and/or practice in some of the countries that now have codetermination systems in operation. There may well now be a general trend towards defining the responsibilities of all board members in terms of the primacy of enterprise as a whole, but having due regard to the interests of both of its two most component parts; that is, capital and labour as well, perhaps, as the public at large.

The Question of Public Representation

Growing out of the former section is the larger question of public representation on company boards. Western European countries have devoted a great deal more attention and effort to the question of worker representation on company boards than to that of public representation. Yet as both labour and management grow more powerful in many of these countries the public may find itself the victim of some of their codecision-making.

To be fair it has to be acknowledged that there has been some movement in the direction of protecting the public interest under various forms of codetermination. Under the Montan and new compromise models in West Germany, for example, the chairman of the board is always an independent and neutral person who often tends to inject some degree of his or her version of the public interest into the proceedings of the board. Some such influence may also stem from the one employee and one shareholder nominee within the Montan system who are to have no connection with the company or union involved. The Dutch mutual-veto model also almost invariably ensures some board members who are bound to reflect their interpretation of the public interest in the board's deliberations. Perhaps most significant of all is the fact that the draft European Companies Statute provides for a co-opted one-third of the supervisory board to represent the general interest, while one of the options available to member states under the proposed EEC Fifth Directive provides that some of the board members may be public representatives. The problem with this approach is that it begs the question of how best to select such representatives — a matter more fully discussed later on in this volume.

The Question of Management Representation

The new West German compromise codetermination model reserves one of the worker representative seats on the board for a representative nominated by the senior executive or management group from among its own ranks, but elected by the salaried or staff employees as a whole. Even if this provision did result from a compromise within a series of compromises, it does raise a legitimate issue that could loom larger in the future. Many levels of management within large corporations have long required representation of some sort to pursue their own concerns, which are sometimes quite distinct and separate from those of the owners, senior managers or workers. Perhaps they will find this representation by joining the unions of those they supervise. A more logical and sensible route for all concerned would probably be for them to form unions of their own.

The point is that their numbers are becoming large enough, and their interests often distinguishable enough, that they would appear to merit their own separate representation within any codetermination system. Assuming this to be the case, their constituency should be much broader than that prescribed in the West German compromise model, and they should be able to decide on their own who should represent them.

Elitism or Formalism

One of the most difficult challenges in attempting to assess the meaning and relevance of various forms of industrial democracy in Western Europe is to distinguish between law and practice. Related to this difficulty is that of ascertaining whether some of the systems involved are more prone to giving rise to a new elite of worker representatives than to dealing effectively with employee concerns.

On the first score, just as many collective bargaining procedures in Western Europe have become so centralized as to lose touch with rank and file worker feelings, so is there a risk that some of the more grandiose industrial democracy models can become quite remote from the shop floor. Codetermination is especially vulnerable on this front because the worker representatives involved often seem so distant and far removed from the day-to-day problems of workers.

Measures have been introduced to reduce this potential gulf. Aside from the fact that most worker representatives on company boards are directly or indirectly elected by the work force as a whole, they usually have their base of political power in the works councils which are in closer contact with the employees. Moreover, in West Germany in particular, these are quarterly mass works assemblies on company time, at which the key worker representatives on the supervisory boards and works councils report on their activities. That even this feedback procedure leaves something to be desired is suggested by the fact that there are thousands of workers in attendance at some of these assemblies.

That supervisory board members and works councillors do at times tend to constitute a new elite of worker representatives is suggested by the many perquisites that often go with their positions. Many of them are released on full-time pay from their regular jobs and have well equipped offices and supporting staffs paid for by the company. In some cases, workers literally have to book appointments with these representatives.

Beyond all this, many worker representatives on company boards are paid handsome director's fees. Together with key works councillors they may also serve on local labour courts and on other public agencies for which they receive extra remuneration.

Since those involved are for the most part elected to their positions, there is this ultimate democratic check should they lose the confidence of their constituents. Various signs of a kind of underground employee representation system in several Western European countries — somewhat akin to the early days of the job stewards' movement in Britain — attest to the fact that even this ultimate check may not be enough to maintain the faith and trust of workers in their representatives at different levels in the industrial democracy system.

It would take a great deal of indepth research to get at some of the signs of worker alienation within some Western European codetermination systems and other forms of industrial democracy. This study has focused on formal institutional arrangements, to the neglect of informal effects and side effects. Caution is thus required in any mention of the latter. That there are real risks involved is undeniable. The question is how serious they are and what can be done to alleviate and minimize them.

CONCLUSION

Despite all the issues and problems involved, worker representation on company boards is likely to continue to spread in Western Europe. Employer resistance to the concept, except in the form of outright parity, is giving way — if only to resigned acceptance. Meanwhile, overall union thinking is gradually moving more in favour of the concept. In some cases, the reason for this interest will remain essentially that of access to information and insight so as to enable more effective collective bargaining. In other cases codetermination will be sought on as full a basis as possible — to complement and supplement collective bargaining, as well as other forms of industrial democracy, and as part of a social partnership between labour and management. In still other and perhaps more significant cases, the far left may well come to accept codetermination as a logical preparatory and transitional step towards its ultimate objective of total workers' control and self-management.

As for the effects of codetermination to date, the major impact appears to have been upon areas of management decision-making which seem likely to impinge upon the income and job security prospects of workers. Employers operating under codetermination systems have had to reconcile their legitimate quest for efficiency and productivity with these understandable concerns of their employees. Beyond this basic type of consideration, codetermination sometimes has had a more obviously beneficial effect on management by reducing the mystery and suspicion that often surrounds the activities of company boards. Codetermination has, in some cases, led to much more appreciation and even sympathy for those charged with the conduct of corporate affairs.

Perhaps the greatest problem with codetermination lies in the fact that it tends to attract too much attention when it comes to worker participation in various forms of industrial democracy. Company board membership for union and worker representatives is clearly of central significance in Western Europe's persistent movement towards more industrial democracy. Yet it is not necessarily the most critical form of this phenomenon. The groundwork for what takes place on company boards which include labour representatives has often been laid at other levels. Very often this spadework takes place at the works council level, where much of the real interaction between labour and management occurs.

Chapter 8

WORKS COUNCILS

A more familiar and older form of industrial democracy than codetermination or worker representation on company boards in Western Europe is to be found in the form of works councils. These councils are sometimes called enterprise councils, works committees, workers councils or by other similar names. Such councils, for the most part, were originally created with a view to providing workers with a form of representation at the plant and sometimes company level, other than through trade unions and collective bargaining which tended to be inactive at these levels. This distinction has become increasingly blurred as works councils have assumed more powers and organized labour has taken a greater interest in their activities.

Despite the central importance of works councils within many Western European systems of industrial democracy, this chapter can be much shorter than the preceding one on codetermination or worker representation on company boards because many of the issues and problems brought out in connection with the latter also apply to the former. The fact that all of these issues and problems are not repeated here is not meant to imply any downgrading of their significance in relation to works councils. Nor does it in any way detract from the critical role that works councils play in many countries, a role which many would argue is in a number of ways more important than that of worker representatives on company boards.

THE POSITION OF WORKS COUNCILS

Works councils may be established by law, by national or local agreement between central or lower level aggregations of labour and management, or largely by employer initiative. Works councils in most countries, other than Britain and the Scandinavian nations, are long-standing statutory bodies which are often older than the unions which exist in the same enterprises. Works councils in most of Scandinavia, by contrast, have in general emerged as a result of agreements negotiated by national labour and management organizations. There are also some works councils in many countries, including Britain, which have been created by employers and organized or unorganized employees outside of any standard framework for such bodies.

Historically one could argue that works councils were created either to fill the void left by the absence of effective trade union organization at the plant or company level in most Western European countries, or to serve a quite different and distinctive representative function. The evidence on balance appears to favour the latter interpretation more than the former. Thus one finds that when most work councils were established they were given terms of reference emphasizing their role in serving the mutual interests of employers and employees through efforts designed to improve the well-being of the enterprise and the welfare of its workers. This is hardly the language of collective bargaining and industrial relations in the normally accepted interpretation of those terms. Rather it is directed towards more consensual, constructive and harmonious relations between employers and employees. Further testimony to the fact that work councils to this day are not intended in many countries to be part of the normal union-management negotiating procedures is to be found in provisions precluding them from interfering in ongoing trade union and collective bargaining activities. Finally there is the fact that unions have over the years been steadily increasing their own separate forms of representation at the shop-floor and enterprise levels.

Except in West Germany and Austria, works councils are joint labour-management institutions usually with the right of equality of representatives from both sides. In West Germany and Austria they are strictly worker organizations, although they meet regularly with employer spokesmen. For practical purposes the distinction between a works council composed entirely of employees and one constituted jointly by labour and management does not appear to be that great, except where the worker representatives have little or no time to caucus or meet on their own.

Works councils represent all the workers in an enterprise in almost every country. Accordingly there is often a form of proportional representation designed to ensure that shop-floor and salaried employees each have their due share of influence. Special arrangements have also been made to ensure that young workers are adequately represented. These arrangements were introduced in response to the crisis years of the late 1960s and early 1970s. Provision has or is now being made in a few cases, notably France, for separate representation for professional workers as well as for lower-level managerial employees.

Works council members are selected in enterprise-wide secret ballot elections which are subject to varying degrees of complexity. These elections are held every three years in West Germany in the spring and receive nation-wide attention. Except in Belgium where unions have the exclusive right of nomination, union influence in these elections is usually limited to the nomination of slates of candidates. That union candidates usually do well in these elections is exemplified by the West German case, where it is estimated that ninety percent of all works council chairmen and seventy percent of works council members are trade union members. This is despite the fact that under forty percent of the paid work force is organized. Even so, this does not necessarily make the works councils subservient to the unions. Although they often work in close concert with each other, they sometimes part company. This is because of the company or enterprise orientation works councils sometimes acquire, even on issues which run contrary to fundamental union policies.

In many instances unions are trying to gain greater control over the functions of work councils by playing a more active role themselves at the enterprise level. This new emphasis by unions has been aided and abetted by a number of new laws in different countries recognizing or strengthening the role and status of union delegates, stewards or trustmen within the enterprise. This often represents a marked departure from past practice, under which there was little or no open union presence at the shop-floor level.

Where required by law, works councils usually exist in non-union as well as union enterprises. They sometimes function quite effectively in unorganized plants, if only because employers envisage them as devices to help them ward off unions and therefore try to make them work to the satisfaction of their employees. Lacking any outside backing, the worker representatives on such councils are normally at a distinct disadvantage vis-à-vis their employer.

WORKS COUNCILS — TRADITIONAL WEAKNESSES

Past union misgivings and reservations about works councils have not only reflected their lack of direct control over them, but an even greater criticism has related to the limited powers of works councils in all but a few countries. Until recently most works councils were limited, for the most part, to certain rights of information and consultation. Beyond this they were normally confined to a restricted list of codecision-making powers over such relatively mundane matters as start-up time and vacation scheduling. In addition they often have complete control over the administration of social or welfare functions — ranging from canteens and day-care centres through athletic, cultural and housing programs to consumer cooperatives and mutual aid societies. The magnitude and scope of these activities in many Western European companies and countries is not to be minimized, especially in terms of their meaning to employees.

As for information-sharing, it has usually been of a broad economic and financial character relating to the past performance and future outlook of the firm. Even then such information is occasionally only made available to special economic committees constituted either quasi-independently of or as subcommittees to the work councils and subjected to stringent degrees of confidentiality. The interrelated nature of the problems posed by union demands for more data disclosure and management concerns about the consequences of such a requirement is of such significance as to warrant a special section in the next chapter.

Consultation in the past normally applied to a much broader range of questions, but was strictly for advisory purposes. Employers were compelled, at the most, in effect, to make work councils aware of their plans in such areas as plant reorganization and technological change. Although obliged to listen to the advice and counsel of their works councils on such plans, employers were free in the final analysis to proceed as they saw fit.

Until recently it was only in a few countries, most notably West Germany, that works councils had very significant codecision-making powers. Thus, in West Germany, for example, even before the 1976 extensions, works councils could in effect preclude management from taking any action in a number of areas until the council was persuaded to go along. Among the areas involved were those relating to appointments, realignment of work groups and transfers of workers, as well as the scheduling of such critical matters as overtime.

Mention should also be made of the role of works councils in wage determination. Except where precluded by law or the national or regional collective agreements in question, works councils have often been highly successful in achieving substantial concessions over and above the minimum rates established by such agreements. The fact that they have frequently been able to do so, even in the face of a peace obligation, indicates that many of these concessions reflected market pressures as much as the negotiating power or skills of the works councils. It is also to be noted that any such concessions have no legal standing and can be withdrawn at any time by employers.

Most revealing of the relative impotence of works councils in many countries is their preclusion from dealing with any matter covered by collective bargaining, unless permitted by the agreement in question to do so. This prohibition reflected union concerns about works councils trespassing on their jurisdictions as much as anything else. This somewhat artificial and unreal demarcation line is beginning to give way in those countries where unions are taking more control over the councils as their powers are expanded. In fact there is a tendency for these developments to proceed in tandem.

WORKS COUNCILS — SOME RECENT DEVELOPMENTS

Currently, works councils in Western Europe are either disappearing or losing influence or undergoing a kind of rebirth or resurgence. Works councils in their original form have almost disappeared from the scene in Italy, where the unions have rejected them in favour of factory committees or delegations. In a few cases both the unions and the works councils have lost out at the plant level where factory councils have emerged as highly independent employee organizations. Many works councils are losing influence in Scandinavia, as the unions become more active and expand the scope of their negotiations at the enterprise and plant levels.

In most other Western European countries legislation has recently been passed to strengthen the position of works councils in virtually every respect. A similar process is occurring by voluntary agreement of the parties involved in a few countries, including some of the Scandinavian nations. Not only are these trends leading to more rights in each of the three spheres of information, consultation and codecision-making but also to a gradual shift in the distribution of such rights from the first to the second and from the second to the third categories.

In the field of information all of the countries involved are requiring that works councils be provided with more comprehensive general economic and financial data. The scope of such requirements is also being broadened to embrace more detailed information about prospective organizational and technological change of all kinds. This enlarged scope tends now to include everything from possible acquisitions, mergers and shutdowns to new plant layouts and products. The trend is clearly toward mandatory revelation of virtually every change that can have an impact on the employment or working conditions of the labour force.

Widened information rights, in and of themselves, lead to more pressure for both additional consultation and codecision-making powers. As for consultation, employers are being increasingly compelled by law and practice to seek the advice and counsel of their works councils in a host of areas previously within the exclusive domain of management prerogatives. Again, in those countries where an effort is being made to revitalize their work councils, almost every matter which can effect vital employees' interests is now subject to some degree of discussion within these councils. Even in France, works councils must now be consulted on such matters as collective dismissals and profit sharing.

Most radical and significant is the less pronounced trend towards granting works councils more codecision-making or veto powers over management actions. In the past such powers were limited to relatively mundane matters, such as holiday and shift scheduling. Currently many more important issues are being brought within this orbit. In Holland, for example, works councils now have an equal voice with management in works regulations, health and safety matters, pension plans and profit-sharing or saving systems. Even in West Germany, wide new codecision-making powers are being extended to its already comparatively influential works councils. These powers now cover recruitment and redundancy policies as well as standards for piecework, bonuses and other payment-by-result systems. A host of detailed individual wage-determining policies have also been brought under joint control in Austria.

On the Western European-wide basis the EEC draft for a European Companies Statute, calling for European works councils within such companies, is suggestive of the shift in emphasis which is taking place.

These councils are projected to have wide information privileges, general consultative rights and extensive codecision-making powers. Besides up-to-date data on the overall economic and financial situation in the company, these councils will have to be provided with detailed information on each of the company's areas of activities and subsidiaries. The councils will, in effect, be provided with more data than is normally made available to shareholders since they will receive, in addition to the company's annual accounts and reports, all the pertinent facts on any change, development or project which could significantly affect the interests of the employees. The extent of this information requirement is underscored by the fact that the council may request a written report from the company on any subject which it feels may have a major bearing on its work force.

Consultation is to take place on the usual range of issues, including all forms of job evaluation, all types of payment systems and any devices designed to control or regulate the pace of work. Consultation is also called for in the case of any major change of any kind likely to have any appreciable effect on the employment or income levels of workers. Management is not allowed to proceed with any changes in these latter areas of consultation without the approval of the council. The council may withhold such approval until a satisfactory adjustment plan has been worked out to alleviate and cushion the impact of the proposed change upon the workers. If no such plan can be worked out by the parties, their differences are to be submitted to third party adjudication by an arbitrator.

Codecision-making — which really would seem to embrace the provision for such social plans — would prevail over everything from recruitment, promotion and dismissal policies, and procedures for the fixing of the terms of individual remuneration, to safety, health and hygiene measures and work scheduling criteria and practices.

Given the range and scope of the proposed European Works Council's information, consultative and codecision-making rights, it is hardly surprising that many trade unionists are as leery about such bodies as employers. What bothers the unions is not only the tremendous potential for overlap between the jurisdiction of such councils and their own collective bargaining activities but also the fact that any such matters could be subject to arbitration — a procedure most Western European labour movements still shy away from, at least when it comes to the resolution of collective as distinct from individual rights disputes.

Yet by far the more basic union objection is the first one, since it raises anew the issue of the relationship between works councils and their procedures and unions and collective bargaining. As works councils are granted more direct control over matters not normally the subject of union-management negotiations, they also require more indirect power over matters that clearly fall within the collective bargaining arena. Take the issue of wage supplements over and above those agreed upon in national or regional negotiations. Even when works councils are subject to a peace obligation, they can use their codecision-making or veto power over a number of critical areas as leverage to extract more local wage concessions. In boom times in West Germany, for example, it has not been unknown for a works council to deny an employer more overtime work until higher wages or other concessions are offered.

FUTURE PROSPECTS

As in the case of the other forms of industrial democracy in Western Europe, it is difficult to find much common ground on the outlook for works councils. About the only thing one can say with some certainty is that more effective instruments for worker representation at the plant and company level are bound to emerge in all countries. Where work councils have acquired a very poor reputation in the past in terms of their effectiveness, as in France and Italy, it may take the emergence of an entirely new body to serve the same purpose as revitalized works councils in many other countries.

The more likely course of action in these countries is reflected in the EEC proposals for Western European-wide works councils in companies which may eventually have the opportunity and choose to incorporate on this basis. As works councils achieve more information, consultation and codecision-making rights they will increasingly take on the characteristics of local unions in North America. This trend will be reflected in turn in even more successful efforts by unions to take them over in all but name.

One effect of this change in orientation will be some movement away from collaboration and cooperation and towards conflict and confrontation. How marked this shift proves will depend on a host of variables, ranging from ideological considerations to the state of individual enterprises and national economies. Some such shift was probably invariable in every country, if only because it is unrealistic to pretend that any level of employer-employee interaction can entail anything less than a changing mixture of common and divisive elements.

Chapter 9

OTHER ISSUES, PROBLEMS AND PROSPECTS

Having dealt with the major forms of industrial democracy now in operation in different countries in Western Europe, it is now appropriate to review some related and supplementary matters. The first of these embraces the concept known as worker asset or capital formation, or more generally as economic democracy. The second covers the other end of the industrial democracy spectrum and deals with the question of shop-floor democracy and the quality of working life. Growing out of all forms of industrial democracy are two critical issues or problems not yet fully explored. One concerns the provision of information to worker representatives and the consequent confidentiality dilemma. The other raises the challenge of education and training adequate to prepare labour as well as management representatives for effective participation in various types of industrial democracy. Finally to be touched upon are the complications raised by the presence of multinational enterprises and the difficulties posed when attempting to introduce industrial democracy in the public service. Some thoughts about the future outlook involved will be offered in each case.

WORKER ASSET AND CAPITAL FORMATION PLANS

A distinction was drawn between economic democracy and industrial democracy in Chapter 2. It is now time to explore the former, which is much less developed than the latter in Western European countries. Economic democracy covers the various means by which workers may be provided with a financial stake, other than in the form of their wages and salaries, in the companies for which they work or in the enterprise system as a whole.

Most of the schemes now in effect and directed towards this end are in the nature of profit-sharing or savings plans. Only recently, has very serious thinking been devoted in a few countries to more advanced or radical asset or capital formation plans. Under these plans workers gain part equity or ownership in an enterprise or series of enterprises through the acquisition of shares either on an individual or collective basis. Indirectly some of the same results may be achieved through varying degrees of union and worker control over the investment funds accumulated under pension plans.

Only when unions and workers acquire control over shares do any of these developments mean very much in terms of industrial, as well as economic, democracy. Even then it is only after they achieve control over a significant proportion of shares in particular companies that they can use this control to influence the formulation of enterprise policies in general.

Profit and Share Participation in France

Ever since 1959 France has been promoting a series of profit and share participation plans through a combination of laws and collective agreements. Under the first such law, tax incentives were introduced to encourage firms to negotiate profit or share participation plans with the unions or work councils representing their employees. Few enterprises or workers took advantage of this opportunity.

A new obligatory law designed to achieve roughly the same purpose came into effect in 1967. It provides for a mandatory share of profits above a certain level, in firms with over 100 workers, to be set aside for collective investment in the name of individual workers, in accordance with terms negotiated with their unions or works councils. Such investments may be in the form of shares or certain fixed return deposits which employees are unable to draw upon for at least five years. Many more employers and employees have obviously been affected by this law than the earlier one.

Increasingly liberal tax concessions have been offered over the years in France to induce the development of more profit and share participation plans. Share distribution schemes have also been promoted particularly actively in a few nationalized enterprises such as Renault. Despite all this encouragement, neither profit nor share participation plans have yet proved that popular in the country. One of the primary reasons for this continuing lack of interest is that the dominant left wing unions view these plans as another device serving to prop up the existing economic order which they are dedicated to toppling.

Government Encouraged Worker Savings and Investments in West Germany

Interest in some form of worker asset or capital formation began in West Germany many years ago in the construction industry. It was envisaged as a kind of substitute for codetermination which did not lend itself to ready application because of the floating, mobile and often transitory nature of both labour and management. Based on the preliminary thinking on such participative arrangements which took place in this industry, the government eventually evolved a plan which can best be described as a form of tax-induced voluntary worker savings and investments. The plan which emerged was eventually designed more to encourage savings as part of an overall anti-inflationary strategy than it was to encourage either asset or capital formation or profit or share participation.

What was enacted in the end was a law which provides employees with financial assistance from the state in support of savings for certain types of investments. Aside from buying shares in companies, such investments were defined to include life insurance and home ownership payments. Up to ninety percent of such investments took place in the latter forms, with less than ten percent being set aside for the purchase of shares. This percentage remained small, despite the added inducement of tax arrangements allowing firms to sell their shares to their employees at very advantageous prices providing the workers retained them for at least five years.

Because of the disappointing progress which was being made under these various provisions, the government came up with a new set of proposals for a more general form of employee participation in the shares of all enterprises. These proposals would have required all firms earning a profit above a given amount to contribute a proportion of the extra sum to a general investment fund for the benefit of all workers. These proposals were dropped in favour of other political priorities before their detailed ramifications could be worked out, and nothing has happened since then. About all one can say at this point is that the labour movement and some of its political allies seem to be maintaining a somewhat dormant and passive interest in some such participation plan, while employers remain leery and watchful lest similar proposals surface again as the economy recovers. The reasons for employer concern in this area are dealt with later in this section.

Denmark's Proposed Wage Earners' Investment and Profit Fund

Early in 1973 Denmark's then Social Democratic Government

proposed the establishment of a Wage Earners' Investment and Profit Fund. This Fund was to be financed by a system of employer payroll deductions gradually rising to the equivalent of five percent. Up to two-thirds of these deductions could be converted into shares in the enterprise from which they were derived in the name of the Fund. Voting rights associated with these types of converted shares were to be exercised by the employees of the enterprise involved.

The remainder of the overall Fund was to be invested under the direction of a Committee of the Wage Earners' Investment and Profit Fund. This Committee was to concentrate its investments in equities and share commanding full capital and voting rights. The degree of ownership of a particular enterprise acquired by this Fund was never to rise above fifty percent. Voting rights for shares acquired by the Fund through purchase rather than through the aforementioned conversion provision were again to be exercised by the employees of the companies in question, except under special circumstances according to which the Committee could assume them.

All workers in an enterprise were to be credited with the same share of their firm's contributions to the Fund. Each employee was to receive an annual certificate to this effect which could not be sold or otherwise transferred for a specified number of years.

These proposals have yet to be acted upon, but interest in them remains high among all but those in employer and conservative political circles. Some variation on these proposals will almost inevitably be introduced at some point.

The Meidner Plan in Sweden

The most far-reaching and revolutionary approach to worker asset or capital formation emerged in 1975 in Sweden in the form of a report prepared by the research director of the Swedish Confederation of Labour (LO) and some of his colleagues.

The background to this report on worker capital formation through collective employee funds is interesting. When the 1971 LO Congress authorized the study, it was clearly motivated by concern over both the concentration of power and the unequal distribution of wealth in the country. As the Meidner Report itself reveals, the LO's own solidarity program had in recent years served to aggravate this concern. The LO had persuaded its higher paid members, and indirectly those of other unions as well, to accept lower increases than they could have extracted in order to raise the wages of low paid workers faster. This unutilized scope for extra wage and salary increases — as it was termed in some union quarters — allowed profitable firms in the boom years of the late 1960s and early 1970s to accumulate what became known as excess or extra profits which they distributed or reinvested in the name of their shareholders. From the labour movement's point of view something clearly had to be done to correct this situation, if only to salvage the concept of wage solidarity.

As a remedy and in the name of rather innocent and innocuous sounding employee funds, the Meidner Report came up with a series of radical proposals which would serve to drastically change the allocation of power and wealth in Sweden in relatively short order. The basic idea is to accumulate collective employee funds through contributions derived from company pretax profits in the form of shares of equivalent value. Contributions of up to thirty percent were envisaged, which would mean that a majority of the shares in reasonably profitable firms could be under the control of these collective employee funds within a decade or so.

Many of the details about the administration and organization of these funds were somewhat vague. Although there would be a fund managed by a central trade union, its power and scope was not made altogether clear. At the enterprise level the funds to be contributed out of profits would remain with the particular company in question, while the equivalent value in shares would be allocated to the individual workers involved. The voting rights of the shares would be held by the central fund which would delegate them to the workers' representatives on the company boards. Workers in Sweden already have a minority of two such representatives, a proportion which would presumably rise as their percentage of ownership increased.

Dividends generated by employee fund shares would not be distributed but rather reinvested or devoted to various cultural, recreational or social programs. Employees would apparently be unable to sell or otherwise dispose of the shares allocated to them under this system. Any benefits they derived would be of an indirect and largely non-financial nature. This lack of direct individual worker payoff reflects the ultimate objective of these proposals, which is collective ownership of all enterprises in the name of democratic control of industry. In this sense the whole plan must be seen as part of the Swedish labour movement's overall strategy for promoting industrial democracy in all of its potential forms.

Although the LO adopted the principle of the Meidner Report, its political ally, the Social Democratic Party, proved a little more cautious on the subject because of the variety of other contentious issues it already had to carry into an unsuccessful re-election attempt. Employer reaction to the Report has been somewhat muted, if only because of the defeat of the Social Democratic government. Employers are worried about both the short-run and the long-run implications of the plan. In the short run they envisage a flight of both domestic and foreign capital. In the long run, they fear the potentially tremendous concentration of power in the hands of a few union leaders which could result from the plan, despite the procedures intended to ensure that local unions and worker representatives have control over the voting rights of shares within their sphere.

It is far too early to ascertain what effect the Meidner Report will have. A broadly representative commission of inquiry has been appointed on the subject, the government has changed hands, and the debate over the issues involved has hardly begun. The only thing one can say with certainty is that some redistribution of capital has now become an accepted or shared value in Sweden. Although employers oppose the Meidner Plan as such, they have conceded the principle of worker asset or capital formation. Their current counter proposal is for a decentralized, individually controlled, tax-induced, voluntary savings plan along the West German lines, but with the resulting investments being channeled exclusively into equity capital. Some compromise will doubtless emerge on this question over the next few years.

Control Over Pension Funds in Britain

Another possible avenue by which unions and workers can gain greater control over companies through their equity capital is via their voice in the management of privately financed and funded employer-employee pension plans. Since such funded private pension plans are much more common in Britain than on the continent, it is the centre of Western European interest in greater union and worker share-control via this more or less indirect route.

Britain is now in the process of providing for the joint administration and operation by labour and management of the funds accumulating under employer-employee pension plans. To appreciate the significance of this development one has to understand the growing role which these massive funds can play in the capital market. As they become a more dominant ownership factor in the private sector, unions and workers may use their input into their direction for a number of purposes. Certainly the passive role which pension fund managers have played in the past in companies in which they have placed large investments is likely to give way to a more activist role with a more labour and/or social orientation.

Conclusion

Labour movements in Western Europe are bound to take a greater interest in worker asset and capital formation plans in the future, as growth and prosperity return to their countries. This interest will increase, despite left wing criticisms that such plans involve the ultimate threat in terms of possible worker cooptation and integration into the existing economic systems. Nor will this interest be deterred by strong employer opposition to such concepts, except in the form of traditional profit-sharing schemes and the like.

What will slow down developments of worker asset and capital formation plans are some of the administrative and organizational problems associated with them. Particularly troublesome is the problem of how and by whom the company shares, acquired under such plans, are to be voted. Even governments sympathetic to labour may prove reluctant to promote such plans, unless effective provisions can be introduced to preclude concentrated union control over these share voting rights.

Assuming this and other related problems can be resolved, worker asset and capital formation plans are almost certain to spread in Western Europe. Visualized as a form of economic democracy they form too natural a complement to the various forms of industrial democracy which are still evolving to be neglected.

SHOP-FLOOR DEMOCRACY AND THE QUALITY OF WORKING LIFE

Much more prevalent than worker asset and capital formation plans in Western Europe are ongoing developments in industrial democracy at the shop-floor level. Although these developments have not been emphasized in this study, they are noteworthy and significant. They are perhaps most important because these forms of industrial democracy usually mean more to workers than the others described in this volume, because they are directly involved in them.

Developments in the field of shop-floor democracy and the quality of working life embrace a wide range of approaches and issues. As to the former, these developments sometimes take the form of new laws and statutes as, for example, in Britain in the case of the Health and Safety at Work Act, or in France where legislation led to the establishment of a national quality-of-working-life centre. In other cases, the impetus for experiments in these areas has come from labour and management. This is especially true in Norway and Sweden. In many instances employers have taken the initiative because of problems ranging from high absenteeism to low productivity.

As for the scope of the issues covered by shop-floor democracy, they include the growing stress which is being placed upon environmental standards for health and safety as well as the host of measures which are being introduced to make dull and routine jobs more challenging and satisfying. In the former area, Britain provides only one example of the trend among countries to take more decisive action to protect workers on the job. Like Britain, the Netherlands has introduced joint labour-management safety committees and empowered union safety representatives to halt work they consider unduly dangerous. Under that country's new democracy-at-work legislation, Sweden's central labour and management federation has negotiated a framework agreement providing for joint safety committees with a labour majority. These committees have jurisdiction over the environmental health and safety aspects of an enterprise's activities. They must be consulted in advance on all proposed new equipment, materials and techniques and, within specific overall financial limits, may decide on further protective measures for health and safety.

As for the nature of work itself and the problem of job satisfaction, managements are continuing to take the initiative in implementing such measures as job rotation and job enlargement and job enrichment. More intriguing is the concept of semi-autonomous work groups which allows relatively small groups of employees to organize and schedule their own work with little or no supervision. Experiments in this area on a joint labour management basis appear to have begun in Norway, but developments in that country seem now to have been outstripped by those in Sweden where the union attitude towards such endeavours remains the most positive in Western Europe. Currently the central labour and management federations in Sweden are working on a framework agreement to govern their activities in this field.

Except where the financial costs involved are high, the forms of industrial democracy just discussed are those most favoured by employers. Basically this is because they appear in many instances to better motivate workers, while posing no serious threat to managerial prerogatives. It is partly because of this favourable attitude on the part of employers that some unions are apprehensive and suspicious about some of these developments. To some trade unionists they are viewed as little more than a new and sophisticated combination of the old Mayo human relations school and the traditional Taylor industrial engineering technique. The use of some types of behaviouralist consultants has often served to heighten and reinforce this impression.

Measures to humanize work and the work place are likely to attract even more union attention than they have in the past. As unions continue to demand and secure more of a joint say in these matters they will become more confident about avoiding management manipulation. The result could be more enthusiastic mutual ventures in this area, as in the case of a number of Swedish companies and plants where it has been discovered that such ventures can pay off in terms of both higher productivity and higher job satisfaction.

INFORMATION AND CONFIDENTIALITY

Employee representatives must be assured of at least three prerequisites in the field of information if industrial democracy is to lead to effective union and worker participation in decision-making. First of all, they must be provided with accurate, complete and pertinent data on the matters to be discussed or the decisions to be taken. Secondly, this data must be presented to them in a comprehensible fashion. Finally, they must be in receipt of the data well enough in advance to make effective use of it.

That employers have sometimes, if not often, been reluctant to provide worker representatives with adequate, clear and timely information is suggested by the increasingly detailed statutory requirements which are appearing in this area. Belgium is an excellent case in point in terms of the elaborate new information requirements it has recently imposed on employers. Belgium's 1973 legislation on corporate information disclosure requires management to provide extensive data on the status of the enterprise, its competitive position, its productivity, its financial structure, its budget and returns, its current programs and future prospects and everything to do with its personal policies and practices. Aside from other data requirements, the law also spells out the manner in which the data is to be discussed, explained and submitted. It also specifies how far in advance some of the data is to be presented and provides for the availability of independent outside experts for interpretative purposes.

Under this law a company can only withhold data if it has a favourable advance ruling from the Ministry of Economic Affairs that the release of such data would be unduly prejudicial to the company's interests. This approach puts Belgium in the forefront of a Western European-wide trend permitting employee representatives to appeal to labour courts or their equivalents to satisfy their claims for information which they feel is being improperly withheld by management. Such tribunals in their work in this area are bound to focus on the central and delicate issue of confidentiality. Some company data may be so sensitive as to merit complete secrecy, at least for a time. This could be a valid argument in the case of proposed new product lines or real estate transactions. Law and practice in other instances may provide for the release of certain data to a few worker representatives for their own exclusive knowledge and use. The confidentiality problem becomes most vexing when release of the information in question could really prove harmful to the interests of the enterprise, while it bears at the same time on matters that are of critical concern to the employees. Anticipated acquisitions or mergers are a classic illustration of this phenomenon.

Where information rights are already fairly extensive there appear to have been few breaches of confidentiality among worker representatives who have been presented with data subject to an obligation to preserve its secrecy. But the issue remains contentious both from the labour and management points of view. Labour wants as much knowledge as possible from management in order to participate on an equal footing, while companies insist that there are some data which they must temporarily retain unto themselves in order to operate effectively. The areas in which employers are likely to be able to preserve such secrecy seem likely to gradually diminish, if not eventually disappear almost altogether.

The ultimate rationale for information sharing is that information in and of itself represents power. Those with the information are always at an advantage relative to those without it. This is why further data disclosure is likely for collective bargaining purposes — as in Britain and Sweden — as well as for other forms of industrial democracy — as in Belgium. Management's continuing effort to prevent the release of data which it legitimately feels must be kept confidential is thus likely to become more and more difficult to sustain.

EDUCATION AND TRAINING

Just as important as information to the effectiveness of industrial democracy is education and training. This applies to employers as well as employees, although the former are usually in a better position to cope with such needs and hence they will be neglected for the most part in this section. More will be said of the fundamental challenge confronting management in this and other areas in the next chapter.

That extensive employee education and training is crucial for industrial democracy purposes is reflected in the growing number of statutory requirements providing for mandatory paid leave for worker representatives serving on works councils or company boards. The West German provisions for these purposes are among the most generous. The first year a worker in West Germany is elected to a works council, he is entitled to four weeks leave for education and training. Thereafter he or she is eligible for up to three weeks leave per year for every year served on the council. Other countries have similar legislative requirements and the trend is clearly towards more liberal leave arrangements for such purposes.

There are precious few examples of union or worker education and training programs which can begin to cope with the requirements called for in most Western European countries. One of the most outstanding jobs in this field is being done by the Metalworkers Union in West Germany (IG Metal) which has one very large and impressive residential college as well as three other smaller ones. This union provides thousands of its members with courses of varying depth, intensity and length. All of its members who serve on works councils and supervisory boards benefit from comprehensive initial programs and annual refresher and updating courses of one kind or another. Only in a few of the Scandinavian countries does one find many unions that can match this kind of effort for their members.

The gap or void left by the general union failure or inability to meet their members' education and training needs for industrial democracy purposes has often been filled by fairly formal and legalistic employer programs directed towards their version of the same end. While there is much to be said for these management seminars for workers, they cannot pretend to serve as a substitute for the kinds of opportunities that unions should be making available to their members. This is one of the reasons why the Bullock Commission recommended modest government subsidies for union programs designed to prepare workers for its version of codetermination. Since governments already extensively subsidize management education and training programs in a host of different ways, it is difficult to quarrel with the notion that they should be prepared to offer similar support to unions and workers.

Such support has been massive in Sweden since the passage of its law placing two union appointed worker representatives on company boards. Under this legislation unions were entitled to a seventy-five percent subsidy for all the relevant education and training they undertook during its first three years of operation. Since then the funding for such programs has been made available through a special levy on the overall wage and salary bill of employers. Most of these programs have been operated on an employer-paid block release basis and have involved almost all the workers now serving on company boards.

Government subsidies of union run education and training programs sometimes lead to questions about the content and nature of such programs. Indirectly, and in a minor way to date, this issue has arisen in West Germany in connection with the statutory leave provisions for worker representatives taking union sponsored courses. Such leave is only mandatory for employees attending courses imparting knowledge necessary for their activities on works councils or supervisory boards. In a few instances employers have challenged the validity of such courses on the grounds that they exceeded these terms of reference and involved anti-employer propaganda.

This raises the issue of the appropriate nature of the orientation of such courses. There seems to be no disagreement about the need to provide some basic knowledge and skills in accounting, economics, finance and other fundamental tools of management. Beyond this more technical side of the education and training required, disagreement begins to arise over such issues as the handling of role conflict and dual responsibilities. Here the management complaint is that union programs often, or at least sometimes, feature the adversarial approach as distinct from those of collaboration and cooperation. Since a mixture of these two sets of approaches is almost inevitable on any joint labour-management body, this is probably not a point to be belaboured.

Given the importance of education and training in any process of industrial democracy the ideal situation would undoubtedly be a combination of union and employer education and training programs for both labour and management representatives, together with whatever separate programs they might each care to offer. There has been some successful experimentation with such joint programs in one or two of the Scandinavian countries as well as elsewhere. Only the extreme and hard-line ideologues on both sides are likely to totally reject such experiments.

THE MULTINATIONAL CORPORATION COMPLICATION

The last two topics of this chapter are among the most controversial of all. The first concerns the handling of multinational corporations and either their headquarters or subsidiaries within national or even international systems of industrial democracy, particularly at the company board level in the form of codetermination. That such corporations do present a serious problem in this context is suggested by the experience of several countries. The most recent effort to cope with this problem is to be found in Britain's Bullock Report. After wrestling with the sundry issues involved, the Bullock majority came up with what they regarded as the least unsatisfactory solution to the problem. On the one hand, they applied their famous $2x + y$ formula to the boards of any foreign subsidiaries operating in Britain with a staff of over two thousand employees. As satisfactory as this might be at the subsidiary board level it would not place worker representatives on the decisive central boards of the multinationals involved over which the country has no jurisdiction. This is the same approach adopted by all Western European countries which now have codetermination systems in effect. On the other hand, they also applied the same formula to the British headquarters boards of multinational corporations having at least two thousand workers in the country itself. This would provide British worker representatives on such boards with a voice in decisions which could have a crucial impact on foreign workers who are in effect disenfranchised for this purpose. This appears to accord with West German experience, but to depart from the approach taken in the Netherlands which exempts holding companies of international groups which have a majority of their employees abroad.

Already noted in several previous chapters have been the EEC efforts to promulgate a European Companies Statute containing several proposals designed to cope with the multinational dimension of corporations. As was seen in these discussions even unions are somewhat leery of some aspects of this initiative, lest they in any way compromise their existing national or proposed international collective bargaining rights.

Multinational corporations are likely to pose problems in the area of industrial democracy as well as many other areas for some time to come. Even in the field of information rights they are still able to hide more than they reveal when it comes to significant issues. Neither OECD nor UN codes of practice are likely to change the situation very much. Just on the information front alone, and solely within Western Europe, it will undoubtedly take the combined influence and powers of the EEC, national governments and a unified inter-country labour movement to make much progress in this area.

Returning to the issue of codetermination or worker representation on company boards, logic suggests only one long-run solution when it comes to multinational corporations. As this form of industrial democracy spreads there should be proportional representation on the headquarters board from all the major countries in which the company has subsidiaries. Where the numbers involved become too large and unwieldy some intermediary body, such as a company-wide work council, would seem to be essential. Those serving as worker representatives on the central company board would probably have to be selected by this body. They would certainly have to take its views into consideration.

At this point a potential problem of some significance could arise between corporate headquarters boards and their subsidiary boards should they disagree on a major issue. The EEC proposal for a European Companies Statute takes into consideration such a possibility and provides that in the event of such an impasse the headquarters board view would prevail — provided it was operating under as advanced a form of codetermination as the subsidiary board in question and included worker representatives from the different countries involved.

INDUSTRIAL DEMOCRACY IN THE PUBLIC SERVICE

Another controversial topic concerns the application of various forms of industrial democracy other than collective bargaining and shop-floor democracy to the public service. Most governments have been somewhat hesitant about introducing works councils — let alone anything like codetermination — in their public services because of concern over the possible impact of such institutions on established civil service regulations and the sovereignty of elected authorities over this domain. Superficially one might suspect a degree of hypocrisy and inconsistency within governments which impose such systems on private employers while exempting themselves from similar complications. Contradicting this interpretation is the fact that there is the potential for major clashes between industrial democracy and political democracy which will have to be reconciled before the most advanced forms of the former can be introduced into the public service.

The need for some caution in this area is suggested by Western European experience with works councils in the public service. Except for the early forms of Whitley Councils in the British public service, works councils have not been noteworthy for their presence in that sector of the economy in Western Europe. Certainly they have never been as common as in the nationalized industries or private enterprises. In the past few years there has been some movement towards removing this discrepancy. For a brief time Germany led the way under its 1974 Personnel Representation Act which established personnel committees in its civil service. Although hardly as influential and powerful as works councils in the private sector, these committees were created to serve many of the same purposes.

Sweden would now appear to be in the forefront when it comes to the application of industrial democracy in the public service. Its new Public Employment Act provides public employees with essentially the same rights as workers in the private sector under the Democracy-at-Work Act. The major difference lies in the fact that the former was not enacted until the unions in the public service agreed to an arrangement designed to avoid and/or resolve conflicts between industrial and political democracy. This arrangement consists of a thirteen person committee composed of seven parliamentarians and three labour and three management representatives from the public service. In the event that any public authority feels that its political sovereignty is being challenged or infringed by any form of industrial democracy it can appeal to this committee for an advisory opinion. Although not binding, such an opinion would doubtless carry great weight. For this reason, both sides in the public service seem determined to avoid such appeals by trying to avoid irreconcilable clashes between industrial and political democracy.

Certainly the Swedish experience in this area will bear watching as the trend towards more and more advanced forms of industrial democracy throughout Western Europe spreads from the private to the public sector. As important as industrial democracy may be, it must not be permitted to reach the stage where it poses a serious threat to political democracy. If a country or society is itself to remain democratic there is no doubt which of the two must prove supreme in the event of a head-on collision between them.

Chapter 10

INDUSTRIAL DEMOCRACY AND THE FUTURE OF LABOUR AND MANAGEMENT

This chapter explores what could happen to organized labour and management in Western Europe if industrial democracy continues to develop along the lines it has been. The first part of the chapter raises the possibility that unions could set the stage for the emergence of something like a corporate state — democratic or otherwise — by seeking too much power at all levels of an economy or society. The second part reviews the impact of continuing developments on the overall industrial democracy front upon the managerial process in general, upon groups of managers particularly at the middle-management level, and upon individual managers at all levels.

TRADE UNIONS AND THE CORPORATE STATE

It may seem ironic and strange to suggest that unions could somehow share the responsibility for paving the way for anything resembling a corporate state, since such a state can so readily develop along lines quite incompatible with the existence of a free labour movement. Yet such a causal link is conceivable and plausible if only because as organized labour seeks a more obvious and open voice in all forms of decision-making in a society it provokes others to demand similar influence, thereby preparing the way for more corporate forms of decision-making.

For present purposes a corporate state may be described as one within which the major economic interest groups either directly or indirectly tend to dominate the determination of all major policies. They may do this in concert with an elected congress or parliament — the majority of which actively and fully supports these policies because it shares a commitment to them. As an alternative, the bulk of such a congress or parliament may become so subservient to the combination of power blocs involved that it has no choice in the matter. The next step could be for representatives of these power blocs to constitute a new assembly or forum which effectively and eventually actually replaces the existing congress or parliament. How much democracy is entailed in each of these stages of possible evolution is an open question. At the very least, direct forms of electoral representation would presumably gradually give way to more indirect channels via the major interest group or groups to which one belonged.

The first move in this possible series of steps depends on the proposition that union power is growing sufficiently to trigger such a sequence of events. There is no doubt that the power of organized labour is increasing throughout Western Europe. Traditionally this influence has been exercised primarily through collective bargaining and political action. Now it is also manifest in the range of other forms of industrial democracy which have been surveyed in this volume. Especially in Austria and West Germany, but increasingly elsewhere as well, the labour movement is making its presence felt in all areas of important decision-making from national economic and social policy formulation to shop-floor democracy. It may also be on the verge of a breakthrough in a number of countries in the field of worker asset and capital formation.

One of the effects of this growth in union power is to drive other interest groups to organize themselves more effectively to pursue their concerns. This is particularly true of employers, again especially in Austria and West Germany, but also in increasing degrees elsewhere. All over Western Europe the fact is that as the labour movement becomes a more potent force, management is compelled to try to establish itself more effectively as an offsetting pressure group. Countervailing power also becomes the object of other interest groups at all levels of society. As this process continues, the government becomes increasingly important as the intermediary power broker — a role which is essential in some form under virtually any system but which can lead to a more corporate form of decision-making if pushed too far, whether by design or inadvertently.

To restate a point made earlier, organized labour, while increasing its powers at all levels of society, has had to engage in a kind of macro-micro tradeoff in terms of its influence at these different levels. In return for more influence at higher levels of decision-making in various countries it has had to compromise its demands at lower levels. It has not given up any of its powers at these lower levels, but it has tempered their application. This suggests that unions can discipline their own use of power, although this only applies as long as those of its constituents who are affected by such displays of self-restraint are prepared to live with the results.

One of the critical challenges which confronts the labour movement grows out of the responsiveness it must demonstrate to its membership's felt and real needs. Each of the three potential ways in which unions may be entrapped by varying degrees and forms of industrial democracy involve compromises to the extent in which they can be responsive to their members' most immediate and pressing interests. As a result these members can become alienated from their unions, a phenomenon which has become quite prevalent even under collective bargaining, the most traditional form of industrial democracy. As long as unions remain democratic, membership alienation can provoke rank and file rebellion — a threat which tends to impose limits on the extent to which unions can display self-discipline.

Another potential check on abuse of union power at various points in society arises from the possibility of a public backlash. There have been signs of such a backlash in several northern countries in Western Europe where the electorate seems to have swung somewhat to the right in recent years. This is, at least in some measure, because of concern over the unduly strong role which organized labour appears to have played in labour and social democratic governments. Assuming that the democratic-pluralistic system remains intact, this ultimate form of check on any group's potential abuse of power will remain critical.

The general public seems quite properly to be suspicious of undue accumulations of power in any one sector of the economy. Industry and commerce have periodically been the subject of effective anti-trust action because of growing misgivings about the amount of power they have acquired. As organized labour assumes more power it too could become even more suspect than it is already in some cases. Concentration of economic or any other kinds of power in the hands of any group can become an intolerable menace to the maintenance of liberal-democratic mixed-free-enterprise systems. Organized labour must remain cognizant of its own perceivable threat to this equation as long as it wants to avoid a confrontation with the public over its power.

The fundamental underlying question is how much power organized labour should want to assume unto itself in the total socio-economic political system. There are at least three interrelated kinds of traps into which the labour movement can fall if it pursues too much influence. The first risk is prone to appear at the company or plant level and is the one most feared by labour's extreme left wing. In more than one context already this risk has come up under the heading of company or enterprise orientation. As organized labour becomes more involved in the policy-making bodies of established institutions, it has to be prepared to live with the fact that its members may more readily accept these institutions. This is the familiar cooptation or integration school of thought and includes the possibility that management may shrewdly manipulate some forms of industrial democracy to serve its own purposes by undermining the loyalty of workers to their unions.

One version of this first risk is also a factor in a second kind of trade union trap, involving the very real possibility that as unions acquire more power they will be virtually compelled to assume more responsibility. The old adage that power begets responsibility is probably as applicable in this area as in any other. There is already ample evidence to this effect in countries with governments supported by and sympathetic to the labour movement. Such governments are frequently more disposed to request and obviously have more of a right to expect an appropriate union response when they require cooperation of one kind or another — more often than not in the form of wage and salary restraint.

The final risk or trap for the labour movement involves the possibility, however remote, of a corporate state evolving out of the trends which are taking place. Much is to be said for some variations of virtually all the forms of industrial democracy which have made so much headway in Western Europe in recent years. But besides entailing more union influence and power they also involve more bipartite, tripartite and even multipartite forms of corporate-like decision-making mechanisms. This may well be the way — even the desirable way — of the future. But it could raise profound difficulties in terms of the maintenance of traditional democratic and pluralistic values. Austrian experience to date suggests that this need not be the case. But Austria is a small country where the bureaucratization and centralization which tends to accompany corporate decision-making has not isolated the system from the people's more direct links with the government via the normal elections for its parliament. Whether other larger countries can proceed as far down the corporate path as Austria has without a conflict and confrontation between power-bloc-corporate and elected congressional or parliamentary decision-making is a moot point.

Suffice it to warn that unions could lose more by a weakening of the present combination of democratic pluralistic and enterprise-collective bargaining systems which now prevail in Western Europe than they might gain under a more corporate form of decision-making. This warning applies regardless of the degree of influence that unions think they might enjoy under the latter. Even the most ardent of trade unions must recognize that there are limits to the amount of power they can wield in any system. Beyond that limit some countervailing power is almost certain to come into play. With this limit in mind the labour movements in many Western European countries might well ponder just how much more power they want to exercise at various levels within the prevailing socio-economic-political systems. Except for those who wish to replace these systems, it is worth stressing that there is probably a rather narrow margin between the maximum utilization of union influence compatible with these systems and excessive use of such power to the point of undermining them.

A final way of emphasizing the point that organized labour should think hard about the overall power it wishes to display in a society arises out of the embarrassment it can cause. Once unions and their political allies are perceived by the general public to be in control of an economy there is no one else to blame if, as and when things go wrong. Britain would appear to be in the process of becoming a classic illustration of this phenomenon almost overnight.

THE FUTURE ROLE OF MANAGEMENT AND MANAGERS

As union influence and power has grown, management interests have felt threatened as never before. Partly because of a decline in their own self-confidence much of management has yet to fashion an appropriate response to the new balance of economic and social forces which is evolving in Western Europe. This confusion is affecting management's collective interest and the manager's individual concerns.

The Pressing Need for a New Managerial Style

Traditional management styles have been rendered obsolete by the combination of a decline in the acceptability of arbitrarily exercised authority and a corresponding growth in the desire for union and worker participation in managerial decision-making. The magnitude of the threat to conventional management approaches is not to be minimized, even though some employers draw some consolation from the apparent lack of interest among many of their employees in some of the more far-reaching types of industrial democracy.

Management's long-standing prerogatives and rights are under assault from so many different directions that they are bound to be eroded even more than they have been so far. Aside from the political front, labour is essentially mounting an effective two-pronged attack on the employers' position. On the one hand, as most fully exemplified by recent Swedish developments, it is greatly widening the scope and thrust of its collective bargaining activities. In most other Western European countries this movement is more subtle and is taking place through the expanded jurisdiction of works councils and their gradual takeover by the unions. On the other hand, as epitomized by West Germany, labour is gaining a greater and more effective voice in all levels of management decision-making. This is gradually occurring from board room to shop-floor levels all over Western Europe. This trend will be further reinforced as various kinds of worker asset and capital formation plans are introduced.

At the very least this combination of bottom-to-top or top-to-bottom union and worker presence in the managerial decision-making hierarchy is ruling out autocratic, authoritarian or paternalistic administrative procedures. Such procedures simply will not be accepted or tolerated much longer in most of Western Europe. The only questions worth asking are what kinds of management approaches or styles will replace them and whether they will be effective in maintaining reasonable standards of efficiency while achieving more advanced forms of industrial democracy.

The answers to these questions are anything but clear yet, but there are some encouraging examples which suggest that this is far from an impossible combination. If more constitutional, democratic or participative management is the way of the future, then it is worth reviewing the experience of the two countries which seem to have moved the furthest in these directions. The best known of these is West Germany, where previous chapters have revealed a fairly integrated overall approach to industrial democracy at virtually all levels of decision-making. Yet the so-called West German economic miracle suggests that effective management has not been sacrificed to any significant extent. So far at least, management has been left with a relatively free hand to operate efficiently, provided it allows for and takes into consideration the effects on workers of literally everything it decides and does. Assuming due allowance is made for their concerns, worker representatives on company boards and works councils do not tend to interfere unduly with management's judgment, as they share the employer's interests in a healthy and prosperous enterprise. Worker representatives may carefully question and scrutinize all aspects of administration and policymaking but, providing they are not incompatible with fundamental union or worker priorities, they do not interfere with or represent an obstacle to general managerial effectiveness and efficiency.

Even more intriguing, but less well-known, is the experience of management in Austria's many nationalized enterprises. In these enterprises codetermination has taken a unique twist which might lead many to believe that management must be completely hamstrung and immobilized. Aside from the one-third worker representatives which serve on the supervisory boards of Austria's nationalized firms, the other two-thirds are made up by appointees of the major political parties in the country proportional to their representation in parliament. Moreover this same proportional representation system prevails across the board on the management boards from which worker representatives as such are excluded. At the supervisory board level this means that major policy decisions can normally be dominated by the worker representatives in concert with the appointees of their political ally, the Social Democratic party. Together, unless the latter are in a distinct minority position in the parliament, they can also exercise a decisive influence over appointments to the management board, provided they respect the proportional political representation which must be maintained on this board.

If one were to judge by Italian experience with political appointees on the boards of nationalized firms one would be inclined to throw up one's hands in despair and to proclaim that such a system could not possibly work. But it does seem to function satisfactorily in Austria because of a combination of historical factors, institutional considerations and values which are peculiar to that country. Neither Austria's labour and management nor its political parties allow their so-called factional approach to the administration of their publicly-owned enterprises to degenerate into the kind of continuous infighting and juggling for position which might occur in many other countries. Instead they use the network of interest groups involved to ensure that they arrive at conclusions which are likely to command fairly universal support.

Austrian and West German experiences are indicative — but indicative only — of where industrial democracy can lead in terms of the managerial process. At the very least, management in Western Europe is going to have to learn to live with more consultation and delays in its decision-making procedures than that with which it is now coping. Beyond consultation and delays there is bound to be much more management by compromise and consensus. Another way of putting it is that the managerial process is certain to become more politicized. This will not only take place in the context of worker participation on company decision-making bodies but increasingly in the context of broader public interests, whether or not they too are reflected in the composition of such boards. Ultimately management by consent of those significantly affected by its decisions may well become the prevailing practice, as now seems to be the case in Austria. Where this may eventually lead in terms of enterprise effectiveness and efficiency is far from clear.

Whither Management Representation?

As the full force and impact of all the developments in the field of industrial democracy in Western Europe strikes various levels of management, it is bound to react more audibly and collectively than it has to date. Just as individual unions of workers organized to counter the undue power of employers, management interests may now have to join together more effectively to counter the growing influence of the labour movement as a whole. Such a response has been delayed, for the most part perhaps, by the diversity of interests that is reflected in the term "management".

At the top of the corporate structure, management may be defined to include the owners or shareholders of an enterprise. Below this level there are the latter's representatives on the company board who may or may not always have views in common with them. Then come the top executives on the management board or some equivalent body. Underneath them are varying levels of senior and middle managers, depending on the complexity and size of the enterprise in question. Finally, there are the first line supervisors or foremen who supposedly represent the dividing line between labour and management. So many levels and types of management are involved — without mentioning the role of key professional groups such as accountants and engineers who are often in a quasi-managerial or staff position — that they often do not share that much common ground.

Most major national employer or management organizations in Western Europe tend for the most part to represent the interests of owners or shareholders and top managers. Even in this limited capacity they often leave much to be desired in terms of their influence and power as an offsetting force to organized labour's central organizations. In part they are at a natural disadvantage, especially in the broad arena of political decision-making, because they obviously have far fewer members of the electorate which they can claim to represent as potential voters for this or that party and what it stands for. These central employer or management bodies in some cases also suffer from inadequate resources and staff, despite the financial strength of their individual members. This is because so many of their member associations or firms — many of which are confederations of associations organized by industry or sector rather than federations of individual companies drawn together along national lines — are still inclined to believe that the main need for concerted action is still at their level. Until these attitudes — vested interests may be a better way of putting it — are overcome, central employer and management groups will remain more handicapped in their activities than they should be. This is unfortunate, not only from the point of view of these organizations themselves and their members, but also because it detracts from the important countervailing capacity they should be mounting within Western European countries to maintain an appropriate balance between national labour and national management centres.

There are some exceptions to the general picture just portrayed. The Swedish Employers' Confederation (SAF) is a relatively strong organization with ample resources and staff. Moreover, it has long maintained a sizable central defense fund and contains within its constitution provisions requiring its members to take strikes or engage in lockouts when it is thought to be in the collective employer interests for them to do so. Heavy financial penalties can be imposed on recalcitrant member firms which decline to go along with such strategies. Recently employers in the Netherlands have also demonstrated an impressive degree of solidarity in the face of union tactics designed to divide them. Aside from one or two other instances, these remain exceptional cases as national employer aggregations remain comparatively weak in most Western European countries.

Equally disturbing, if not more so from a management point of view, is what is happening at the senior and middle manager levels in many Western European countries. The distinctive and separate interests which they have has already been alluded to in the earlier chapter concerning worker representation on company boards. These groups are feeling ever more neglected in the total scheme of things. In varying degrees in different countries they seem to be suffering from a relative decline in both their influence and their incomes. In several countries some forms of industrial democracy are also making them feel more exposed and vulnerable. With those they supervise securing ever more access to even higher levels of management through works councils and worker representatives on company boards, those caught in between are increasingly liable to criticism from above and below. If it has no other effect, this tends to undermine whatever independence and status this group may have enjoyed in the past.

Often feeling apart from and let down by top management, they seem to be in a quandary as to which way to turn. This is reflected in the ambivalence of some of the organizations to which they belong; such as the British Institute of Management which periodically engages in a convulsive introspective debate about whether it should continue to represent the professional interests of management or convert itself into something resembling a trade union in everything but name. Even where senior and middle managers have formed bodies which more aggressively and openly pursue their concerns, as in Belgium, the Netherlands and West Germany, they tend to be relatively impotent bodies unless they can align themselves with more influential groups. In West Germany, to cite an example involving a relatively high level of such managers, they would never have obtained their own representation on company boards had it not been for the compromise codetermination bill forced upon the minority Social Democratic government by the Free Democrats with their managerial and middle class orientation.

Of late, independent managerial unionism may have made its greatest advances in the Netherlands, where it began as a series of house unions in a number of large multinational corporations. After the mainstream of the labour movement in the country decided on a policy of Swedish-type wage solidarity which would have compressed all wage and salary differentials, these house unions formed the nucleus of what can be loosely translated as the Netherlands Central Organization of Higher Level Personnel. Although many, if not most, of the members of this new trade union organization are white collar clerical and lower level supervisory personnel, it is dominated by middle managers and professional staff members. It has become an agressive independent third trade union force working solely on their behalf, lacking as it does any political, religious or traditional labour affiliations.

Lacking any other effective institutional outlets for their frustrations, middle managers (as well as some of their more senior colleagues) are likely to turn to established unions largely out of desperation. In some countries — Belgium is a case in point — they will end up in special unions of their own, but affiliated to the rest of the labour movement. In other cases — Britain illustrates this category — they will be divided up among a host of competing unions claiming jurisdiction because of existing craft or industrial dividing lines. Where this happens there will be little or no chance for the management groups involved to assert their own special interests because they will be such a small minority — and a minority among those over whom they are supposed to exercise direct or indirect supervision on a day-to-day basis.

The general trend is such in Western Europe that neither the owners of enterprises nor various levels of managers are likely to be as effectively represented in the overall socio-economic-political decision-making processes as they should be. This is much less of a problem at the capital or equity level than it is among the different layers of management. The latter groups, as well as many professional elements, play a much more important part in the economy and society in general than is currently or likely to be reflected in the forseeable future in key policymaking bodies at all levels in the overall system.

A Note on Labour Directors and Their Equivalents

In the chapter on codetermination the potentially difficult role of labour directors in the Montan or coal and steel industries in West Germany was highlighted. Subject as they are, in terms of both their appointment and reappointment, to a veto power by the workers' representatives on the company boards, they can be in a compromising position on the management board. The way in which most labour directors have resolved this largely unavoidable conflict-of-interest dilemma seems to have been to recognize it squarely and to play a role openly as a kind of conciliator or mediator or honest broker between the interests of labour and management.

As various forms of industrial democracy at the company and plant level spread throughout Western Europe there will be an increasing need for an institutionalized role of this kind; whether it be in the name of a West German-type labour director or something akin to this position. This has already happened to labour directors in other German industries and is more prevalent than is appreciated in most Western European countries. Industrial democracy cannot continue to evolve in a workable fashion at the enterprise level without more management specialists to resolve role conflicts and dual loyalties and responsibilities. As was indicated in an earlier section on education and training, there are capacities and qualities that more and more managers of all kinds are going to have to acquire and put to use in their daily work.

Chapter 11

IMPLICATIONS AND RELEVANCE FOR NORTH AMERICA

Even the staunchest defenders of the North American collective bargaining system as the most appropriate form of industrial democracy for the United States and Canada will admit that it has many failings and shortcomings. Perhaps most indicative of these weaknesses is the fact that the governments of both countries have felt compelled within recent years to impose temporary wage and price controls.

Being far from perfect, industrial relations in North America could undoubtedly benefit from some of the experiences of Western European countries in this field. The difficulty is that, generally speaking, the North American and Western European industrial relations systems are so different that it is hazardous, to say the least, to think in terms of anything like directly transferring or transplanting basic institutional arrangements either way. Rather, where it seems appropriate, the emphasis must be placed on adaptations of some of the more successful Western European experiments in industrial democracy to fit the North American setting.

This is the approach adopted in this chapter which examines each of the major forms of Western European industrial democracy which have been explored in this survey in the light of their possible application in North America. The focus throughout will naturally tend to be more on Canada than on the U.S. because of the author's background. Such a focus is also appropriate because of the greater likelihood of Canada embarking on some government-induced experiments in Western European-style industrial democracy.

REFORMING NORTH AMERICAN COLLECTIVE BARGAINING

It is well to start with a few thoughts about possible reforms in North America's collective bargaining systems before turning to those Western European forms of industrial democracy which are still quite alien or foreign to North America. This is an appropriate starting point, if only because collective bargaining is likely to remain the mainstay of North American industrial democracy for the foreseeable future. This is doubtless as it should be, given the relatively satisfactory performance of this system over the years. At times it may be too conflict-ridden or inflation-prone, but these attributes also apply to many Western European industrial relations systems.

That the collective bargaining procedure in North America has much to be said for it is underscored by the fact that many Western European unions are attempting to emulate some of its more attractive features. Even where the North American collective bargaining process is fairly concentrated — as in those few cases where effective industry-wide negotiations prevail — the process is in closer touch with rank and file aspirations and concerns because of the local basis upon which most unions are erected. This greater association with the membership is the envy of many Western European unions where priority is now being given to the establishment of a more obvious union presence at the enterprise or plant level.

Having made this comparison it may appear to be something of a contradiction to suggest that the North American system of collective bargaining is in many ways too decentralized and fragmented. But in some industries this is clearly the case; as for example in construction where over twenty unions may be represented on one site with differing conditions and terms of employment. North America obviously is not ready for anything approaching West Germany's comparatively tidy industry-by-industry national and regional bargaining — let alone Swedish-style national framework bargaining — but it could stand a great deal of realignment and restructuring. The only way to achieve this result may be by adjusting the appropriate bargaining units which labour relations boards have decreed in the past on the basis of now obsolete circumstances. The British Columbia Labour Relations Board in Canada is now empowered to reconstitute such units where they have become inappropriate due to changing conditions, and has done so in few situations. Many more private and public initiatives along these lines will be required to begin to rationalize many of the collective bargaining arrangements which now prevail in North America. Such initiatives are not just required to improve the performance of the collective bargaining process in the U.S. and Canada. They are also required to better enable labour and management to take advantage of more advanced forms of industrial democracy should they decide to move in this direction.

At least two other areas should be mentioned in the field of collective bargaining narrowly defined. Both involve highly contentious issues where the trend of events is likely to run counter to coveted management positions. They can best be brought out by suggesting that collective bargaining is unlikely to remain as central to North America's approach to industrial democracy as it is today, unless unions are provided with more information heretofore generally held back from them and the scope of negotiations is widened. On the information front it is noteworthy that

Britain was in the process of providing for the release of more pertinent employer data to unions for collective bargaining purposes even before the Bullock Commission on codetermination began its proceedings. All over Western Europe unions are in receipt of more relevant enterprise data than is the case in North America. Sometimes they receive this data directly as a matter of right, and sometimes only indirectly via union or worker representatives on company boards or works councils. As North American trade unionists become more aware of the comparative paucity of information they have to work from in their negotiations, they are bound to demand similar treatment to that of their Western European counterparts. At some point it is safe to predict that present North American practices, which tend to allow management to withhold all sorts of data from unions and workers on the grounds that it is too confidential, are going to give way to much more liberal information requirements.

At the same time it is equally likely that the scope of collective bargaining will continue to broaden in North America. Such a widening process has been taking place gradually over the years. One only has to look at the range of matters which the National Labour Relations Board in the United States has slowly but surely brought within the gambit of mandatory negotiable issues to appreciate how far this process has already moved. In both the United States and Canada, unions are now negotiating over problems that were hardly thought to be bargainable several years ago. Employee dislocation and disruption brought about by technological and other changes are now governed much more by collective agreements than was the case a decade or so ago. So also are work environment standards, especially in relation to the health and safety of workers.

As noted earlier in the case of Western Europe, broadened information rights tend, in and of themselves, to foster a widened scope for bargaining. This link is likely to follow just as logically in North America as in Western Europe. Past North American notions about confidentiality of information and exclusivity of employer residual rights are bound to prove increasingly passé in any and all areas where vital employee interests pertaining to their income, security and working conditions are involved.

To conclude this section it must be stressed that the most fundamental challenge confronting the North American collective bargaining system appears to be one it cannot possibly meet without some dramatic and drastic changes among both employers and unions. The idea of a free collective bargaining system functioning almost oblivious to national economic and social developments and priorities is becoming increasingly untenable. Yet neither employers nor unions in North America are really prepared for anything else. Instead they engage in a largely uncoordinated and unrestrained dog-eat-dog free-for-all over the spoils of different plants, companies and industries as well as the overall income distribution of the two nations involved. Under present circumstances governments and the public at large seem helpless in the face of these struggles, unless the entire economy is threatened by the process. In that event wage and price controls may be clamped down upon it.

A more enduring and intelligent way must obviously be found to bring some degree of compatability between labour and management wage and price setting procedures and government fiscal, monetary and related policies. The two sets of mechanisms involved cannot continue on their often distinct and separate courses without setting the stage for more frequent and serious collisions between them.

NATIONAL ECONOMIC AND SOCIAL POLICY CONSULTATION

Both the U.S. and Canada leave much to be desired in terms of their present arrangements for national economic and social policy formulation. Either that or the implementation of existing policies is so faulty that this is where the shortcoming lies. In Canada public disenchantment with the general state of current economic and social affairs reflects many highly visible problems which have led to a decline in confidence and a rise in uncertainty. Highlighting these problems are a sluggish rate of growth and unacceptably high rates of both inflation and unemployment. Related problems range from continuing underutilization of the country's capital stock, labour force, natural resources and productive potential; through excessive and misdirected government interference and intervention in more and more areas of the nation's economic affairs; to an industrial relations system unduly disposed to contribute to both conflict and inflation.

While the U.S. performance is better in some of these respects it is much worse in others. It has an even more inequitable distribution of income than Canada's, and yet lacks a social security system adequate to begin to cope with the needs of its most disadvantaged and downtrodden citizens. For one of the wealthiest countries in the world to deny its people universal health care is almost a national scandal in itself. Given these and other basic flaws in the U.S. economic and social fabric, its urban ghetto slums can hardly avoid spawning crime and violence on a frightening scale.

It would be the height of naiveté to suggest that providing labour, or even labour, management and other groups, with a more effective input into national economic and social formulation could contribute that much to resolution of these problems, even on a realistic time scale. Yet such an input is certainly required to try to achieve a set of policies better directed towards the attainment of lower rates of inflation, higher levels of employment and more rapid economic growth — not to mention a fairer distribution of income. If the joint or sundry activities of unions and employers are to mesh at all with those of government aimed at such a combination of goals, then labour and management must have a voice in the process.

Except on an ad hoc basis in a crisis, neither the U.S. nor the Canadian governments are inclined to engage in meaningful consultations with labour and management other than on a highly informal basis. Not even the Economic Council of Canada — from which the Canadian labour movement has temporarily withdrawn in protest over the government's wage and price controls — fills the need, despite its highly representative character. The Council's mandate precludes it from focusing on immediate or short term problems and prospects. Moreover, even when it has something concrete to say about longer term issues, its advice is seldom heeded. In part this neglect of its counsel doubtless reflects the absence of any direct government presence. The short-lived Canadian Industrial Relations Council — from which labour also withdrew over the controls — included a government component and thus was potentially truly tripartite; but it had a mandate which tended to confine it to the industrial relations sphere.

What is needed in Canada — if not in the U.S. as well — is some form of national economic and social consultative body made up largely of labour, management and government representatives; but also including a few other representatives from such groups as consumers, farmers and professionals. This should be a purely consultative body before which the government puts its views on the course of future developments in the country, and the various interest groups reply in kind. If such a process only produced some agreement on the underlying data and basic trends, that would be progress enough for a start. Hopefully it would lead to more than this if the government was less secretive about its annual budget proposals and labour, management and other interest groups were more frank and open about their own plans.

The problem in Canada — and to a lesser extent in the U.S. — is that decision-making in every sphere, and particularly in collective bargaining, is so decentralized and fragmented that any sort of national economic and social planning is difficult to conceive of, let alone implement. Neither organized labour nor management — nor in Canada's case, government — could commit themselves to any concerted action or even consensus on the part of all of their affiliates, levels or members because they do not have sufficient control over them. But somewhere in between some elementary agreement on a common set of data for decision-making and some form of planning could lie some fruitful middle ground for exploration.

Perhaps all that can be hoped for in North America is a national forum other than congress or parliament as a whole before which critical national issues can be thoroughly aired. In that case the U.S. already has such a body in the form of the Joint Economic Committee of the Congress, which serves as the focal point for an annual debate and discussion based on the report of the President's Council of Economic Advisors. Much could doubtless be done to improve this Committee's work, and lacking anything better the Parliament of Canada would do well to provide a similar forum.

In response to the Canadian Labour Congress' recent manifesto calling for an effective national tripartite forum, the Canadian government might well be advised to establish an economic and social council along the lines of the EEC body which bears a similar title. If the government does not want to involve itself directly in the proceedings of such a body, it should be willing to consult it on major policy changes it is contemplating. Initially these issues should perhaps be confined to a limited number of areas. If and when the council acquires more credibility as an advisory group, its consultative range could then be broadened. Canada has very little to lose and perhaps much to gain from embarking on such an experimental undertaking.

Two points should be made in conclusion. The first is that the resistance of the civil service bureaucracy and its top mandarins to such an approach could be great. Much of their power lies in the information they are able to withhold from others and the close contacts they maintain with the prime minister's office, senior ministers and other influential politicians. They are not likely to give up the comparative advantages they enjoy in these respects without a determined backroom fight.

The other more important point to be stressed is that it would have to be made clear from the outset that regardless of the form of any national economic and social consultative body it would have to be limited to an advisory (albeit hopefully an influential advisory) capacity. No government of any stature could afford to delegate its final responsibility for the development of policy proposals, and no congress or parliament should ever abdicate its ultimate authority and power to decide on final policy to such a body.

LABOUR AND MANAGEMENT AND PUBLIC ADMINISTRATION

Little or no thought has been given in North America to the concept of a major, let alone predominant, role for labour and management in the administration of any public programs. Neglect of this concept is apparent even where the parties together both pay for the programs in question and derive the primary benefits from them. This neglect does not just apply to broad overall social security programs such as old age pensions, but to the whole labour market and manpower area as well.

Even in the field of unemployment insurance and in the related areas of placement, training, upgrading and vocational guidance, labour and management are usually limited to a more or less perfunctory advisory role. Most of these matters come under the exclusive domains of large centralized bureaucracies within even more stultifying overall civil service regimes. Sometimes the only saving grace in this context results from the fact that the provinces or states have jurisdiction over all or part of the matter in question. Where this is the case, it is unfortunate that a lack of decent minimal common standards may pose an even greater problem than centralized bureaucracy at the federal level.

Neither the U.S. nor the Canadian record in the fields of most forms of social security is that impressive. Again, particularly in the area of labour market and manpower programs, there are many grounds for concern. Both labour and management complain about a variety of shortcomings in these spheres; although seldom are their criticisms identical, if even similar, in nature. The time is long overdue in Canada, at least, when employer and employee spokesmen should be given a greater voice in the administration of these types of programs. On an experimental basis some aspects of the country's labour market and manpower programs should be placed under a tripartite form of supervisory control. The effectiveness of many of the programs involved could hardly be lessened and might actually be improved under such an approach.

Civil service resistance to such a change-over might be minimized by providing the unions of the employees affected with part of the government's share on the tripartite administrative body. As for the possibility of the government losing control over the situation, this could be minimized by ensuring that this body operated within a statutory framework containing the key features of the programs in question. Basic policy would still remain a legislative matter, but its implementation would be under tripartite direction.

If joint labour management or tripartite administration of public programs does not appear feasible for the time being in any other areas, at least it should be tried in the field of arbitration, conciliation, mediation and other types of industrial conflict resolution. This is a field of critical mutual concern to union and employers, and there are few reasons why they should not be granted greater control over it. Britain's experience to date with its tripartite-managed Advisory Conciliation and Arbitration Service is most encouraging in this regard.

UNIONS AND WORKERS AND THE COMPOSITION OF COMPANY BOARDS

To date North American unions have demonstrated little or no interest in the concept of codetermination or worker representation on company boards. This lack of interest is largely to be explained by the confidence and faith which they have developed in their collective bargaining procedures. For the most part their reliance on these channels has proven highly successful in the attainment of their objectives, which still remain relatively straight-forward in terms of improved wages and working conditions for their members. Lacking any deeper ideological or philosophic commitments, at least at the corporate level, they have been reasonably satisfied with what may be described essentially as a system of challenge and response.

To these considerations must be added the fact that most trade unionists in North America still look with some suspicion upon any form of codecision-making with management, except through collective bargaining itself. Most U.S. and Canadian unions so cherish their freedom of action and independence from management that they are reluctant to contemplate anything that might compromise this position. In its most extreme form this posture precludes virtually any collaborative or cooperative undertakings with employers outside of the normal collective bargaining framework.

Any number of developments could change these traditional union attitudes. Greater familiarization with what is actually going on in Western Europe could have some effect. Heightened awareness of some of the limitations in the collective bargaining process which were mentioned earlier in this volume could prove more telling. But even then a Swedish approach might be sought to solve the problem, thereby leaving it to the parties directly involved to work out their own particular codetermination arrangements subject to some minimum standards. As already indicated, more information and a broader scope for negotiations might be enough in themselves to alleviate, if not eliminate, many of the aforementioned limitations.

Despite their historical lack of interest in anything like codetermination, some North American unions have lately shown some signs of interest in the prospect. In a few cases union or worker representatives are already sitting on some nationalized or public corporations, if only in token numbers. In at least two instances, one involving the highly influential United Automobile Workers and the other the Oil Chemical and Atomic Workers Union, the initial list of demands placed before a major corporation — in one case Chrysler and in the other Shell Oil — have included a proposal for at least one union nominee on the company board of directors. These proposals appear to have been dropped early in the ensuing negotiations, but they could signify the beginnings of a marked shift in union opinion on this question.

In the case of Canada the only significant initiative on this front appears to be coming from the federal government. As part of its effort to re-establish some rapport with the labour movement — which was shattered by the imposition of wage and price controls — one of the proposals the government has advanced is to promote some experimentation with codetermination in its crown corporations. It appears to have taken this initiative without any encouragement from the

Canadian labour movement, which so far seems to have largely ignored the offer.

Although the concept of codetermination is receiving a great deal of attention in Canada, it appears to be no more of a priority issue for organized labour than in the U.S. All in all this is probably a fortunate situation, as there are many aspects of codetermination which would have to be thought through very carefully before they were introduced in North America. The issues involved would not be dissimilar to those which continue to characterize the many versions of codetermination which are now either in effect or in the formulative stage in Western Europe.

One of these issues, which could prove even more hazardous in North America than Western Europe, is that relating to the company or enterprise orientation which can envelop union and worker representatives involved in such schemes. Given the pragmatic bread and butter instincts of the average trade unionist and worker in North America, there is the very real danger that codetermination could in some instances become synonymous with collusion. Safeguards would have to be built in to ensure that labour and management did not use codetermination to conspire jointly against the consumer and the public.

If the composition of company boards is a problem in North America, it is hardly because they lack union and/or worker representation. Far more serious is the absence of any public representation on such bodies. Even if such representatives were only granted a voice and not a vote on major company boards they could perform a useful watchdog role. In such a capacity they could be charged with the responsibility of issuing an annual report on the stewardship of the company in question in the light of existing laws of the land, advertising claims and warranties, and applicable codes of ethics. Hopefully consumer associations and other public interest groups will eventually become sufficiently qualified, representative and strong to provide a source for public members on corporate boards. If the challenge of public representation on large corporate boards is not dealt with on its own merits, it will almost certainly become one critical facet of any codetermination debate which occurs in North America.

If codetermination becomes a major issue, it is to be hoped that North America will proceed by the Scandinavian experimental route before either the U.S. or Canada entertains any across-the-board approaches to this question. In this context nationalized or public corporations would be as good a place as any to begin such experiments.

AN ALTERNATIVE TO WORKS COUNCILS

The issue of Western European-style works councils is largely irrelevent to North America unless a case can be made for them in unorganized enterprises. This is because the labour movements in the U.S. and Canada are based on a foundation of local unions which for the most part adequately serve the needs of workers at the office or plant level. Works councils in Western Europe were initially established in most countries, in part at least, to fill the gaps left at that level by unions which tended to concentrate their efforts on national and regional bargaining. Currently, it will be recalled, unions in Western Europe are pressing hard for a more forceful and influential presence in plants — either by taking over existing work councils or creating rival bodies under their own auspices.

There is only one fundamental sense in which there may be a need in North America for some variation on the Western European works council set-up. Throughout their history, works councils have been intended to play more of a consensual then a conflictual role. Although this balance has been shifting lately, there is still a basic underlying element of cooperation involved in the activities of many of these works councils. In contrast, local unions in North America tend to lean much more towards the adversarial or confrontational end of the consensus-conflict spectrum. This means that North American unions tend to neglect any common interests they may have with employers, while zeroing in on their differences.

There are a few classic examples to the contrary which suggest that local unions can find some middle ground in their relations with employers. Perhaps the most famous of these is the Kaiser Plan which was modeled after the more long-standing Scanlon Plan. The latter essentially involves a labour-cost-of-production savings plan in which workers are provided with a meaningful financial incentive in return for helping to reduce the labour-cost component of total costs. In effect they are offered a bonus proportionate to the increases in labour productivity they help engender. To facilitate this objective there are shop level, plant-wide and, where appropriate, general company production committees where all matters of mutual concern beyond those dealt with in collective bargaining are discussed. Where the Scanlon Plan has worked well, management withholds virtually no data, deals with all questions raised, but retains unto itself final decision-making powers beyond those areas covered by the collective agreement. The Scanlon Plan is usually incorporated into this agreement as it is to be applied to the enterprise in question. The union or unions involved are thus partners to the plan, a partnership which is officially recognized in their right of separate representation in all production committees.

The Scanlon Plan is hardly a panacea to be held up as the best way to introduce a cooperative as well as a confrontational element into the North American industrial relations system. Nonetheless, it does illustrate one reasonably successful way in which this can be accomplished, at least in small and medium size enterprises. As such it exemplifies a variation on the Western European works council approach which can be combined effectively with North America's normal collective bargaining procedures. In this respect it represents a potential supplement to U.S. and Canadian negotiating arrangements, which can add a further element of industrial democracy to the employer-employee relationship.

ORGANIZED LABOUR AND PENSION FUNDS

Like Britain, the U.S. has moved and Canada is in the process of moving towards joint labour-management administration of the vast funds accumulating under negotiated private pension plans. Since such pensions are in reality a form of deferred wages, labour has just as much of a right to a voice in the investment of these funds as management. Although this does not constitute worker asset or capital formation in the newest Western European sense of this concept, it can serve some of the same purposes envisaged by advocates of such plans.

Before turning to these purposes, it should be noted that neither labour nor management in North America has a blemish-free record when it comes to their participation in the administration of pension plans. Continuing revelations about abuses by the Teamsters in the operation of their members' pension plans attest to the violations of trust to which unions can become party. The practice by some employers of investing pension funds under their control in low-yield bonds of their own or associated enterprises reveals that management too can be party to conflicts of interests in this area. The same practice tends to occur in government-run pension plans to the extent that they are funded.

Although joint administration of such plans is supposed to avoid these kinds of problems, this is not always the case. The acquiescence, if not acceptance, by employer trustees of some of the fraudulent practices engaged in by their Teamster union counterparts is most disquieting in this regard. Even when the fiduciary responsibilities involved are laid down fairly precisely, as they are under the applicable U.S. legislation, they are not always well adhered to or enforced. Also discouraging is the low level of competence of many labour and management trustees of pension plans, due to their lack of education and training.

Where jointly administered pension funds do not suffer from any dishonesty or fraud — which appears to be the case in the vast majority of cases — the trustees on both sides seem to concentrate on making the shrewdest investment decisions possible. Within the legal constraints which bind them, they seek out a combination of the potentially most profitable and risk-free investments available. For the most part, they seek and take the advice of professional pension fund managers who generally operate in a highly business-like and ethical manner.

What has to be stressed, so far at least, is that labour and management trustees of pension funds concentrate on making the best possible investment decisions for the eventual beneficiaries of these funds. Most significant of all is the fact that union trustees have brought little pressure to bear to develop any other criteria for these decisions. Neither have they sought to channel such funds into labour or socially oriented projects nor have they tried to use the voting power of the shares they half control to influence managerial priorities in the companies in question.

That labour will acquire growing leverage over many corporations via its voice in the administration of pension funds holding large blocs of their securities is not to be denied. The question is whether union trustees will ever get together to coordinate their potential leverage in these areas. Assuming they do, there is the larger question of how they will deploy that leverage. It is likely to be some time before this leverage is used in North America to do anything other than further more sound returns on the investment of the funds in question.

HUMANIZING WORK AND/OR THE WORK PLACE

North American unions have yet to show much interest in such concepts as shop-floor democracy and the quality of working life. To a large extent U.S. and Canadian unions have more or less assumed that work is by its very nature unpleasant, and that the best approach is to seek more and more pay for less and less of it. This approach has long been tempered by concern about the most uncomfortable, unhealthy and unsafe environmental features of the work place; but only recently in a few quarters have unions begun to concern themselves with the nature of work itself.

The fact that non-union firms have often been in the forefront of North American efforts to humanize work and the work place has not helped the situation. In most of these cases there is no doubt that these efforts have been part of a calculated employer strategy designed to maintain their non-union status. The fact that this strategy often seems to pay off for a mixture of reasons (of which such approaches as job enlargement and job enrichment are only one) has not lessened union concern about some of the motives behind such efforts.

Now the federal governments of both the U.S. and Canada are becoming more active in this field. The U.S. has created a government agency within the executive branch of the federal government known as the National Quality of Work Centre. The outgrowth of a series of such bodies which began with more emphasis on productivity than the quality of working life, the new Centre has shifted the balance decidedly towards the latter. It has regional offices which are promoting a range of approaches designed to improve job satisfaction and, hence it is argued, efficiency as well. The Canadian government is now in the process of establishing a similar body on a quasi-public basis under multipartite direction.

As employers and governments have taken more action in these areas, there has been a gradual but perceptible change in the attitude of some unions. The United Automobile Workers (UAW) has been in the forefront of this change, if only because some of the major companies with which it deals were promoting a number of quality-of-working life experiments. The UAW's cautious acceptance of these experiments was reflected in its 1974 agreements with the big three automobile manufacturers. These agreements provided for the establishment of special national joint union-management committees to assess the results of the experiments which had already taken place and to encourage more mutual experiments in the future. Despite these agreements or perhaps because of them, the number of such experiments seems to have diminished in the past few years.

Because the UAW is probably North America's most progressive union, anything it does is almost bound to have considerable significance.

The fact that it is now willing to accept the possibility that there is something to the quality of working life movement is certain to influence the thinking of other unions. Even so, the North American labour movement's skepticism about developments in this general area is likely to persist for some time to come. What unions in both the U.S. and Canada will certainly insist on is an equal voice in whatever takes place in the name of humanizing either work or the work place or both in any enterprises under their jurisdictions.

EDUCATION FOR INDUSTRIAL DEMOCRACY

To end this chapter a word or two is in order about the need for more education in all forms of industrial democracy. Even if collective bargaining remains the primary focal point of industrial democracy in North America, a strong case can be made for more education and training of those directly involved in the process. The case for such education and training will become all the stronger as various other forms of industrial democracy evolve in the U.S. and Canada — if only in such fields as the maintenance of higher environmental standards for health and safety in the work place.

As was noted in an earlier chapter, employers tend to be further ahead in the education and training of managerial personnel than unions in the case of their representatives. This is primarily due to the greater financial resources at the former's disposal. Rather than offsetting this advantage, current government policies in both the U.S. and Canada tend to aggravate it. This is because general government spending on education and training is directed almost exclusively towards forms of schooling more useful to employers than unions. As is now occurring at the federal level in Canada, it is time all levels of governments in North America provided organized labour with more direct and indirect assistance for its educational and training efforts.

Some of this assistance should be provided in forms which encourage more joint labour and management efforts in the field of education and training. This is especially necessary where the latter is directed towards preparation for more advanced forms of industrial democracy. Since part of the purpose then to be served would be to further more labour-management cooperation, there is no better place to start than in the laying of the initial groundwork for such cooperation.

Chapter 12

SUMMARY AND CONCLUSION

This volume has reviewed the many forms of industrial democracy which are either in operation or under serious consideration in various Western European countries. This survey was conducted with a view to ascertaining the relevance of these concepts to North America, bearing in mind both the need for improvement in its industrial relations and the general differences in the patterns of these relations on the two sides of the Atlantic.

Not surprisingly it became quite apparent in most instances that, while many Western European forms of industrial democracy have proven highly effective in certain settings, they are not readily transferable to others. Nonetheless there is something to be learned from all of them, even in North America where the circumstances are so different from those in Western Europe that great care would have to be taken in attempting any such transplants. At best the most which could be introduced in the U.S. and Canada are carefully adjusted adaptations of successful Western European ventures in the industrial democracy field.

It is not without interest that this could and should be a two-way process. Although North America doubtless has more to learn from Western Europe when it comes to various types of industrial democracy, the former also has something to offer the latter in some areas. Western European experience in industrial democracy is to be found at all conceivable levels of interaction between labour and management. In this sense it can be said to be well ahead of North America. But unions in the U.S. and Canada remain much closer to their members than their counterparts in most Western European countries. In the long run this is a critical relationship, the nature of which can make or break any system of industrial democracy.

It remains to review three matters. The first of these is the often complex and delicately-balanced combination of attitudes, institutions and processes which together represent the prerequisite for effective forms of industrial democracy. The second concerns the appropriate nature of the route to forms of industrial democracy beyond or other than collective bargaining. Finally, a few thoughts are offered about the choices which lie ahead, both in the fields of industrial democracy in particular and in industrial relations in general and in the related but wider socio-economic-political sphere.

THE PREREQUISITES FOR EFFECTIVE FORMS
OF INDUSTRIAL DEMOCRACY

Either in concert or in combination most forms of industrial democracy tend to depend on a common set of conditions for their successful implementation and operation. Although fulfillment of all of these conditions is not essential to the functioning of industrial democracy at any level, it is hard to imagine a well-integrated overall system working without them. In contrast, most of the conditions mentioned are hardly essential to the functioning of a simple and straightforward collective bargaining procedure, albeit perhaps a highly strife-ridden one.

Even collective bargaining depends upon a degree of ideological compatability between organized labour and management, although the threat of protracted industrial disputes can bring about temporary settlements between the most divided of protagonists. Extreme ideological and philosophic differences are less compatible with forms of industrial democracy which entail something more than collective bargaining. This is because such forms normally are based on the proposition that there is some common ground between the parties involved.

On the side of organized labour a high degree of pragmatism is usually required. This does not mean that individual unions or the labour movement as a whole need give up their more political or reform-minded objectives. But it does mean that they must temper them, at least to the point of being willing to work within established orders. Attempts to radically and rapidly transform such orders are likely to prove difficult to reconcile with meaningful forms of industrial democracy.

As for employers and managers there are at least two pre-conditions. The first is full acceptance of a legitimate role for trade unions at the various levels of decision-making affected. The second is management on a far more open and participative basis than in the past. Neither autocratic nor paternalistic approaches to administration are appropriate when compromise, consensus and politics become more commonplace.

Both employers and unions must nevertheless be strong if they decide to engage in different types of industrial democracy. For one or the other to be weak is to tempt its opposite number to manipulate the situation to its undue advantage. Just as collective bargaining depends on a reasonable balance of power between labour and management, so also do other forms of industrial democracy.

There must also be a frank acknowledgment by labour and management of the combination of mutual interests and natural differences that is basic to their interrelationship. Seldom do the parties have any difficulties recognizing their inevitable points of disagreements. These are what brought organized labour into being in the first place. Usually both sides also know that they share or ought to share some common objectives. The problem for each is to admit this unavoidable fact of industrial relations life to the other, and then to act jointly upon that mutual understanding.

If industrial democracy is to become a basic operating premise in any society it is useful, but not vital, that it function at all levels of that society. West Germany provides the best approximation of a totally integrated overall approach to industrial democracy. This can best be illustrated by briefly reviewing the various ways in which labour exercises its influence at different levels of decision-making in that country.

Aside from the fact that over fifty percent of the members of the West German Bundestag or Parliament are trade unionists, the West German labour movement has other important channels through which it can influence national economic and social policy formulation and its administration. Organized labour in West Germany has an equal voice with management in the country's Concerted Action Committee which, although not as significant as when it was established, still is available for high level tripartite consultations when they are deemed necessary. In addition, West German labour shares with management control over the public corporations which administer virtually all of the country's man-power and social security programs.

Within individual companies West German labour has varying degrees of influence and power within what are currently the most highly developed forms of codetermination at the corporate board level. In addition West Germany's works councils, especially at the plant level, have a more determining voice in what goes on at that level than equivalent bodies in most comparable countries. In the field of shop-floor democracy and the quality of working life, West German labour again has joint control with management over the large amounts of funds which the government has made available to the parties for experimental undertakings.

In and of itself this brief review illustrates the prerequisites for successful Western European experiences with various forms of industrial democracy beyond collective bargaining. It tends to bring out some of the difficulties which would arise in North America should either the U.S. or Canada choose to pursue some of these forms. Dealing first with the attitudes of the parties most directly involved there are problems on both sides. As for organized labour in North America, it is certainly as pragmatic as its Western European equivalent — indeed, in some respects, much more so — but its very pragmatism could be a serious impediment to progress in any of these areas. It is so cognizant of its adversary or opposition role vis-à-vis management that it is dubious, skeptical and suspicious about any kind of relations with employers other than through collective bargaining.

Employers have contributed to this hostile union attitude in a number of ways. Historically, they have resisted the inroads of organized labour in every way possible. Many large employers still remain non-union and intend to continue that way. Unionized firms jealously guard their prerogatives and rights and fight every assault on them. Legal as these strategies and tactics may be in North America, they hardly contribute to a climate more conducive to cooperative and collaborative relations with organized labour; although some such relations do exist in a few instances.

Even if organized labour and management were desirous of new types of relationships, they would be handicapped institutionally in the extent to which they could readily change or shift direction. They suffer from few such handicaps at the enterprise or plant level, where they have highly developed interrelationships. The major problem would arise at higher levels where meaningful links between unions and employers are more noteworthy for their absence than their presence. Especially at the national level there is a great gap or void between organized labour and management. Not only is there comparatively little contact at this level, but that which does occur is largely of an informal and superficial character. Even if such contacts were to go further, they would mean very little, as neither labour nor management centres in North America have any power to commit their affiliates or members to anything of significance. Both their constituents continue to guard their autonomy extremely jealously, and would not give much of it up lightly — if at all.

Assuming industrial democracy were ever to amount to anything very significant at the higher corporate or industrial and national decision-making levels in North America, Canada would find itself in even more difficulty than the U.S. On the corporate side this is because so much of Canadian industry is dominated by multinational corporations headquartered outside the country, primarily in the U.S. Codetermination and other forms of enterprise industrial democracy are likely to prove far less meaningful when the basis of corporate power lies abroad. On the governmental or national side, decision-making in Canada is complicated by a federal-provincial system which is growing ever more decentralized due to unrelenting nationalist pressures from Quebec and complementary demands for more power from some of the other provinces.

All in all, North America hardly represents fertile ground for experiments in industrial democracy between labour and management — let alone between labour, management and government. North America never experienced the unifying postwar reconstruction crisis that Western Europe did. Nor has the U.S. or Canada any real tradition of cooperation or collaboration between labour and management. Partly as a result of its own unique background and history neither unions nor employers are equipped institutionally to participate in industrial democracy ventures beyond the local level. Yet attitudes doubtless remain the really crucial issue. Should labour and management in North America mutually decide on a different course of action they could in time no doubt bring it about. Until then it is unrealistic to expect any significant change in orientation.

THE ROAD TO INDUSTRIAL DEMOCRACY

If new forms of industrial democracy do come to represent a realistic option for North American unions and employers, the way in which they are introduced could prove critical. Despite the U.S. and Canadian tradition of detailed and exhaustive legal intervention in the collective bargaining sphere, this may not be the most appropriate way in which to proceed when it comes to other forms of industrial democracy. Certainly it would be most unwise to legislate mandatory statutory requirements in this area until labour and management are more interested and better prepared for it. Cooperation and collaboration are hardly the kinds of relationships which can be mandated by legislative fiat.

The types of industrial democracy in question do not involve such basic emotional issues as trade union recognition, which reactionary, recalcitrant and retrenched employers in North America refused to concede until they were compelled to do so by law. Rather what is at stake is the way in which labour and management should conduct their relations once they have been established. So far at least, most unions and employers in North America appear reasonably content with their present collective bargaining arrangements. Until one or the other or both are otherwise inclined, it makes little sense to try to force them to accept new interaction mechanisms.

It is at this point that a word of caution and warning is in order. North America may already be in the process of being overrun by numerous under-informed (if not completely ill-informed) advocates of Western European-style industrial democracy. Among these almost missionary-like advocates are academics from different disciplines, civil servants within all kinds of government bureaucracies, journalists in every branch of the media, and politicians of many strains and varieties. Relatively few of these well-meaning missionaries have any practical experience in either labour or management, let alone in the realities of collective bargaining and industrial relations. Those among them who have had such experience more often than not have fled it for a more relaxed and sedate career outside of the labour-management arena.

Unions and employers in North America would be most unwise to voluntarily accept or lightly acquiesce in the imposition of any new forms of industrial democracy upon them until they have had a chance to see for themselves how they work in practice. It is in this spirit that more undertakings, like the UAW's sponsorship of a trip by some of its members to work within a Swedish plant featuring semi-autonomous work groups, are in order. Preferably visits such as this should take place on a joint labour-management basis, so that they can mutually assess the possible relevance of various forms of Western European-style industrial democracy to their particular circumstances. Nothing short of this kind of joint study trip should suffice before labour and management in North America embark on experiments in these areas.

Together with other measures, some forms of industrial democracy other than collective bargaining could doubtless do much to help solve some of North America's industrial relations and socio-economic-political problems. It would be the height of irrationality, however, if such forms of industrial democracy were to be imposed on reluctant unions and employers. If only out of respect for the underlying concept it embodies, industrial democracy should be introduced more voluntarily than by decree. There may eventually be a role for the latter, but only after the general principles involved have become so widely accepted by labour and management that it is a case of inducing the holdouts to move along with the mainstream of developments. Even then legislative or statutory approaches can but encourage such a process. There are limits to the extent to which unions and employers can be compelled or forced to get along better on any basis.

THE CHOICES AHEAD

It is questionable whether North America's present industrial relations system can continue without some basic reforms. The socio-economic-political challenges confronting the U.S. and Canada are serious enough to warrant the consideration of alternative approaches in every part of the overall system. The collective bargaining procedure is as deserving of review as any other facet of the prevailing order. Some adjustments are probably inevitable in this sphere, as in all other areas of North American life.

Changes in the system could all too readily become unavoidable with the only real issues tending to revolve around their direction, magnitude and speed. The answers to these questions may well hinge on whether the changes come by design or default. There is a very real danger that they will come by default of the existing system, rather than by the calculated and reasoned design of those most directly affected. Hopefully any changes will come by the latter route, in which event there would seem to be three or four alternative courses of action from which to choose.

The first of these options would involve the reform and revitalization of North America's present industrial relations system in conjunction with appropriate changes in the entire socio-economic-political system. Basically this approach would entail reinforcement of the best features of what's left of the so-called free collective bargaining and free enterprise systems, together with measures designed to alleviate or eradicate their more disturbing features. Essentially this in turn would only require a strengthening of the checks and balances which now are intended to preclude any one interest group from acquiring and utilizing too much power. There is no organized power bloc in the U.S. or Canadian economies and societies which should not be subject to more vigilant scrutiny. Where any such bloc is found to be taking undue advantage of other groups or the public in general its position must be countered, undermined or weakened by a wide array of anti-combines or anti-trust like measures. There is no other way to tackle the competitive, institutional and structural imperfections which plague North America. Beyond this fundamental need a more efficient and humane social security system will have to be developed. Other necessary refinements include those mentioned earlier to bolster the effectiveness of the present collective bargaining process. The essential point is that none of these requirements are that radical or revolutionary, although there would be considerable resistance to many of them.

A second option grows out of the developments discussed in this survey. If economic and social power blocs are to continue to grow in influence and strength, then new ways must be found to ensure that their interaction leads to results which are reasonably compatible with the general public interest. As far as labour and management are concerned, this doubtless means that they would have to learn to interrelate in forms other than conflict-oriented collective bargaining. It is in this context that some modified versions of Western European-style industrial democracy could become much more relevant to the North American scene. If this happens, much more provision should be made for some public input into the processes involved than has thus far been injected into these processes in Western Europe. Otherwise some of the procedures could all too readily lend themselves to collusive labour-management practices running counter to the public interest. Lacking any more effective form of representation, this element in the total system tends to be represented solely by government which could find itself wielding a heavier and heavier hand in the total system.

This suggests a third and fourth pair of options: one more or less tolerable but fraught with great risk; the other, which could easily grow out of the first, quite unacceptable in terms of its incompatability with the fundamental underlying values of the North American way of life. As for the former, it has already been described as a democratic corporate state along the lines of that which now prevails in Austria. Involving a combination of private power bloc and congressional or parliamentary decision-making, this approach embodies the ready acceptance and even encouragement of such blocs while incorporating them into the total system.

The danger is that this deceptively appealing approach can give way to a less democratic process as control over the overall system becomes more bureaucratized and centralized. Although concentrated power may lead to the exercise of more responsibility by the various groups possessing such power, it may also lead to an intensive struggle over which of them is to have the decisive say in its application. The notion that power can corrupt may override the fact that it can also lead to more responsible behaviour.

North American society, and especially Canada, is subject to many forces and pressures for change. These are eventually bound to be reflected in the industrial relations arena as well as in all other areas of decision-and policy-making. Somewhere in between North America's romantic old-fashioned view of free and unfettered collective bargaining and the ultimate threat of an undemocratic corporate state lies a reasonable and realistic accommodation between the U.S. and Canada's present collective bargaining system and Western Europe's various forms of industrial democracy. The challenge for labour and management more than anyone else is to discern that accommodation and to work towards its implementation.

That the stakes involved are of momentous consequence is not to be denied. If unions and employers continue to rely on conflict and confrontation as the basic force behind their relationships, they will continue to set the stage for more and more unilateral government intervention. Although this threat is now more readily apparent in Canada than in the U.S., it is no less real in the latter than in the former. If labour and management are to continue to have the major say in their mutual destiny, they must build up more consensual relations to complement their natural and unavoidable conflictual ones.

The ultimate choice now beginning to confront all modern industrialized societies is between highly bureaucratized and centralized corporate and technocratic systems and a series of reasonably well balanced and interdependent quasi-autonomous sub-systems. Collective bargaining could prove to be one of the first of these sub-systems of democratic pluralism to be jeopardized if the choice even begins to go the wrong way. For this reason labour and management could be risking everything if they do not consider more carefully, earnestly and openly all of the alternatives which are still freely available to them.

Selected Bibliography

Asplund, C. *Some Aspects of Worker Participation*. Brussels: International Confederation of Free Trade Unions, 1972.

Barkin, Solomon, ed. *Worker Militancy and Its Consequences – 1965-75*. New York: Praeger Publishers, 1975.

Batstone, Eric and Davies, P.L. *Industrial Democracy: European Experience*. London: Her Majesty's Stationary Office, Two Reports Prepared for the Industrial Democracy Committee, 1976.

Business International S.A. *Industrial Democracy in Europe: The Challenge and Managerial Response*. Geneva: Business Interional S.A., 1974.

Commission on Industrial Relations, *Worker Participation and Collective Bargaining in Europe*. London: Her Majesty's Stationary Office, C.I.R. Study No. 4, 1974.

Commission of the European Communities, *Employee Participation and Company Structure*. Brussels: Commission of the European Communities, Bulletin of the European Communities, August, 1975.

International Labour Office, *Collective Bargaining and Industrialized Market Economies*. Geneva: International Labour Office, 1973.

International Labour Office, *Workers Participation Within Undertakings*. Geneva: International Labour Office, Labour Management Relations Series No. 48, 1976.

Kendall, Walter, *The Labour Movement in Europe*. London: Allen Lane, 1975.

Malles, Paul, *The Institutions of Industrial Relations in Continental Europe*. Ottawa: Information Canada, 1973.

Organization for Economic Cooperation and Development, *Workers' Participation*. Paris: Organization for Economic Cooperation and Development, Documents Prepared for an International Management Seminar, 1975

Walker, Kenneth F. "Workers' Participation in Management — Problems, Practices and Prospects". In *Bulletin of the International Institute for Labour Studies. pp. 3-35. Geneva: International Labour Office, International Institute for Labour Studies, No. 12, 1974.*

Index

Advisory Conciliation and Arbitration Services (Britain), 76-77, 157
AFL - CIO, 33, 40
Attitudes towards work, 18-19
Austria: industrial relations in, 41, 42
  Parity Commission for Wages and Prices, 63-64
  management of social security systems, 77-78
  codetermination in, 96, 143
  works councils in, 116
  management in nationalized enterprises, 143

Belgium: bargaining practices in, 46
  labour involvement in social and economic policy, 66-67, 69
  management of social security systems, 77
  legislation on corporate information disclosure, 128-29
Biedenkopf Committee (West Germany), 88, 89, 90
Britain: industrial relations system in, 40, 58
  "social contract" in, 58-61, 69
  Advisory Conciliation and Arbitration Services, 76-77
  joint labour-management administration of pension plans, 125-26
  labour-management safety committees, 127
  see also Bullock Commission
Bullock Commission (Britain), 92-95, 99, 101, 102, 105, 131, 132, 152
"Business union" option in collective bargaining, 7

Canada: industrial relations system in, contrasted with that in U.S., 39-40
  economic problems, 153
  need for a national economic and social consultative body, 154-56
  interest in codetermination, 158-59
  problem of multinational corporations, 169-70

Canadian Industrial Relations Council, 154
Canadian Labour Congress (CLC), 33, 40, 155
Capital formation plans, *see* Economic democracy
Class conflict model for industrial relations, 40, 41
Codetermination: in West Germany, 17, 83-90, 94, 95, 142-43
  union attitudes to (Europe) 20, 21-23, 80, (North America) 157-59
  employer attitudes to, 24
  attitudes of EEC member governments to, 25
  in the Netherlands, 90-92
  Bullock Report (Britain), 92-95
  Sudreau Report (France), 95-96
  Austria, 96, 143
  Scandinavian countries, 96-97
  European Economic Community, 97-99
  continuing issues and problems in, 99-108
  effects of, 108-109
  and multinational corporations, 133
  North America, 157-59
  Canada, 158-59
Codetermination Act, 1976 (West Germany), 86-87
Collective agreements, 15
Collective bargaining: traditional model, 6-7
  alternative approaches, 7-8
  in North America, 15-16, 36, 150-53
  limitations of, 20-21
  in Western Europe, 36-37, 45-52
  and works councils, 111, 112, 115, 117, 118
  see also Dual level of bargaining, Framework bargaining
Collectivism in Western European economic system, 29
Company boards: worker representation on, 80-109, 157, 158, 159
  unitary and two-tier, 81-83, 101, 102
  public representation on, 105-106, 159
  management representation on, 106-107

see also Codetermination

Concerted Action Committee (West Germany), 64-66

Confidentiality of corporate information, 129, 130

Consensual model for industrial relations, 25, 40
in Australia, 42

Corporate state, 55, 137-41, 173, 174

Denmark: proposed Wage Earners' Investment and Profit Fund, 122-23

Dual level of bargaining, 36-37, 45

Economic and Social Committee of the European Communities, 69-70

Economic and Social Council (France), 67

Economic and social policy consultation, (Europe) 54-70, (North America), 153-56

Economic Council of Canada, 154

Economic democracy: definition, 14, 120
and industrial democracy, 14
profit and share participation in France, 121
worker savings and investments in West Germany, 121-22
Denmark's proposed Wage Earners' Investment and Profit Fund, 122-23
Meidner Plan in Sweden, 123-25
problems associated with, 126
joint labour-management administration of pension plans, (Europe) 120, 125-26; (North America) 161-62

Education and training (Europe), 130-32, (North America), 164

"Elitism" among worker representatives, 107-108

Employers: attitudes to industrial democracy, 23-24, 128
differences between North American and Western European, 35-36
attitudes required for successful forms of industrial democracy, 167, 168, 169, 170
in France, 42
increasing organization as reaction to union power, 138, 144, 145
see also Management

Environmental constraints on industrial relations: differences between North America and Western Europe, 28-32

Eurocommunism, 30

European Companies Statute (proposed), 98, 106, 133
proposals for European works councils, 116-17

European Economic Community, 21, 24-25
and codetermination, 97-99, 155

Federal Employment Institute (West Germany), 74

"Fifth Directive" on European company law (proposed), 98, 99, 106

Foundation of Labour (Netherlands), 61, 62

Framework bargaining, 46

France: duplication of employee representatives, 33-34
industrial relations system in 41, 42
bargaining practices in, 46
interest-group participation in economic and social development, 67, 69
labour and management involvement in administration of social security programmes, 77
profit and share participation plans, 121

Free enterprise system, 11, 28

Government: role in traditional collective bargaining system, 7, 16
interest in industrial democracy, 24-25
in Western Europe, contrasted with the North American situation, 30, 31
differing roles in industrial relations in Canada and U.S., 39-40
involvement in framework bargaining in Scandinavia, 46
and formulation of national economic and social policy, 54, 55
as power broker in the corporate state, 138

Grievances, 37

Hierarchy of needs, 18-19

Individualism in North American economic system, 29
Industrial conflict: differences between North America and Western Europe, 37-38
Industrial relations: rapid change in Western Europe, 8-10
contrasts between North American and Western European systems, 28-43, 150
variations within North America, 38-40
variations within Western Europe, 40-43
Information: provision of, to works councils, 114, 116, 117
and workers' participation in decision-making, 128-30
and multinational corporations, 133
provision to unions, 151-52
Interaction processes in industrial relations: differences between North America and Western Europe, 36-38
Interest groups: and formation of public policies, 54-55
in the corporate state, 137-38
Italy: industrial relations system in, 41
collective bargaining trends in, 48-49
social security administration in, 77
works councils in, 115

Joint Economic Committee of the Congress (U.S.), 155

Kaiser Plan, 160

Labour courts: tripartite administration of, 72-73
Labour directors, 85, 87, 147-48
Labour movement, involvement in politics, 15-16, 56
participation in national economic and social policy formulation, 17, 54-70, 153-56
Canadian contrasted with U.S., 40
role in public administration, 72-78, 156-57
attitudes required for successful forms of industrial democracy, 167, 168, 169, 170
see also Unions

Labour Party (Britain), 58, 59, 95
Labour relations boards, 31
Law: role in industrial relations, 31-32
Liberal democracy, 10-11

Management: role in public administration, 72-78, 156-57
representation on company boards, 106-107, 146
need for a new managerial style, 141-44
organizations, 145, 146
position of middle and senior managers in industrial democracy, 145-46
unions for, 146-47
labour directors, 85, 87, 147-48
see also Employers
Manpower: involvement of labour and management in administration
of programmes, (Europe) 73, 74-76, (North America) 156-57
Meidner plan (Sweden), 97, 123-25
Montan model of codetermination West Germany, 84-86, 87, 88, 89, 105, 106, 147
Multinational corporations: and industrial democracy, 132-34
in Canada, 169-70

National Council of Labour (Belgium), 66
National Economic Development Commission (Britain), 60
National Labour Market Board (Sweden), 74-76
National Quality of Work Centre (U.S.), 163
Netherlands: involvement of labour in national economic and social policy, 61-63, 69
Social and Economic Council, 61, 62, 90, 91
administration of social security programmes in, 77
codetermination in, 90-92
works councils in, 116
labour-management safety committees, 127
managerial unionism in, 146
New Democratic Party (Canada), 39

North America: industrial relations in, contrasted with Western European systems, 28-43
variations in industrial relations system of, 38-40
reforming collective bargaining in, 150-53
economic and social policy consultation, 153-56
role of labour and management in public administration, 156-57
codetermination, 157-59
works councils, 160-61
joint labour-management administration of pension funds, 161-62
humanizing work and the work place, 162-64
education for industrial democracy, 164

Parity Commission for Wages and Prices (Austria), 63-64
Parties of interest in industrial relations: differences between North America and Western Europe, 32-36
Pension funds: joint labour-management administration of, (Western Europe) 120, 125-26, (North America) 161-62
Politics: involvement of labour movements in, 15-16, 56
contrasts between North America and Western Europe, 30-31
Profit sharing, 120, 121
Public administration: role of labour and management in, (Western Europe) 72-78, (North America) 156-57
Public representation on company boards, (Europe) 105-106, (North America) 159
Public service: industrial democracy in, 134-35

Quality of working life, 126-28, 162-64

Scandinavian countries: codetermination in, 96-97
works councils in, 115
see also Denmark, Sweden
Scanlon Plan, 160-61
"Shop-floor democracy", 126-28, 162-64
Social and Economic Council (Netherlands), 61, 62, 90, 91

"Social contract" in Britain, 58-61
"Social programming" in Belgium, 46
Social security programmes: involvement of labour and management in administration of, (Western Europe) 73-76, 77-78, (North America) 156-57
Sudreau Report (France), 95-96
Sweden: capitalism in, 29
changing industrial relations in, 43
collective bargaining trends in, 49-51
participation of labour in national policy formulation, 67-69
National Labour Market Board, 74-76
codetermination in, 97
Meidner plan, 97, 123-25
joint safety committees, 127
industrial democracy in the public service, 134-35
Swedish Employers' Confederation (SAF), 145

Trade Union Congress (Britain), 58, 59

Unions: alternatives in collective bargaining, 7-8
challenges to, in Western Europe, 9
and political action, 15-16, 56
attitudes to codetermination, (Europe) 21-23, 80, (North America) 157-59
differences between North American and Western European, 33-35, 47 in Austria and West Germany, 41
in France, 41, 42
in Italy, 48, 49
conflicting pressures on, in Western Europe, 47
in Sweden, 49-51
control over worker representatives on company boards, 104-105
and works councils, 113, 117, 118
attitudes to humanizing of working conditions, (Europe) 128, (North America) 162-64
education and training programmes, 130-32, 164
and the corporate state, 137-41
growth of power, 138-41
for management, 146-47
see also Labour movement
United Automobile Workers (UAW), 163-64

United States: industrial relations system in, contrasted with that in Canada, 39-40
economic and social policy formulation, 153-54, 155
National Quality of Work Centre, 163
see also North America

Wage controls, 55, 150, 154, 158
West Germany: Concerted Action Committee for economic and social planning, 64-66
manpower and social security administration in, 73-74
codetermination in, 83-90
works councils in, 114, 116
worker savings and investments in, 121-22
management in, 142-43
integrated approach to industrial democracy, 168
Work: attitudes to, 18-19

alienation from, 19
humanizing of, 126-28, 162-64
Worker asset plans, *see* Economic Democracy
Worker control, 17, 22
Worker representation on company boards, *see* Codetermination
Works councils, 111-18
selection of members, 113
and unions, 113, 117, 118
and collective bargaining, 111, 112, 115, 117, 118
traditional weaknesses, 114-15
consultative and codecision-making powers, 114-15, 116, 117, 118
recent developments, 115-18
in the public service, 134
North America, 160-61
mentioned, 17, 20, 91, 92, 130

Yugoslavia, 17